Fat Skeletons

URSULE MOLINARO lives in New York City. A
writer and translator (of Herman Hesse, Christa
Wolf, Philippe Sollers, Nathalie Sarraute, Dino
Buzzati and others), she is author of ten novels
including *Positions with White Roses* and *The New
Moon with the Old Moon in Her Arms* as well as a
number of highly-praised short-story collections.

Fat Skeletons

Ursule Molinaro

Serif
London

First published 1993 by
Serif
47 Strahan Road
London E3 5DA

British Library Cataloguing-in-Publication Data.
A catalogue record for this book
is available from the British Library.

ISBN 1 897959 02 8

Photoset in North Wales by
Derek Doyle & Associates, Mold, Clwyd
Printed and bound in Great Britain by
Biddles of Guildford

A translator in Greenwich Village
notices alarming similarities
between her own Prague childhood
and a "brilliant novel" by a rising
young star of Czech literature.

She's in the bathroom brushing her teeth, when the phone rings. She catches it on the fourth ring, before the machine picks up. & wishes she hadn't when she hears his voice, informing her that: she sounds funny.

She probably does, with a mouth full of toothpaste.

Although   hasn't he noticed?   that her voice always turns funny, that her voice recoils, when he calls.

Which he does three, maybe five times a year. Usually to propose an 'ethnic' dinner in a cheap neighborhood. Which is all a poor writer like him can afford. A pure writer, who doesn't compromise to suit a market.

A pear-faced old souse, who tells the novels & stories & articles he doesn't write. To other deaf ego-cocoons in cheap neighborhood bars.

For twenty years she has recoiled from his voice on the telephone. Accepting one out of three to five ethnic-dinner invitations when she feels particularly sick of an author she's translating. Vicious enough to replenish her self-esteem by comparison to Mandy Murdoch. Her careful make-up & chic haircut to the genteel pear face across from her, that is thirstily absorbing the wine she always brings to these discoveries of his. These holes in the wall that have no liquor licence. She may not have written the novel she came to America to write twenty years ago, but at least she has become a widely respected, sought-after translator.

Of novels other Czechs have written. In their native, reader-restrictive Czech. About life in Czechoslovakia, which they are too committed   or too fearful   or otherwise unable to leave. For a distant, reputedly free country, where a different sound reality assails the exiled writer's language. & new images produce a different story.

At least she's earning her keep.

Then, as the label: TRANSLATOR turns back into the hated obstacle that has been standing in the way of her own writing

—not only taking up all her thinking time, but also blinding any editor against looking at a work of her own: She's the TRANSLATOR, a middle person, expected to turn foreign books into American bestsellers. When they sell, everyone praises the author. When they flop, everyone blames the translation—

she smirks at the pear face across the table from her. That is reading her an article he actually wrote   last night, or ten years ago   smiling at words or passages he deems particularly felicitous. About some deceased Has-Been he used to know. & drink with. Who used to admire the stories/novels/memoirs he used to tell him. But who   unlike him   did most of *his* writing on paper.

She isn't listening. She has heard him read enough of his stuff to know that she likes neither his self-tender narrative, nor his preoccupation with the past. She's asking herself, as she always does, during these dinners, WHY she continues to see him. Or listen to him on the telephone. Just because twenty years ago, a woman she no longer sees, & has little desire to see again; ever —a contact her mother made for her, pulling apron strings all the way across the Atlantic; the editor who contracted her first translation; of one of her mother's novels— brought Mandy Murdoch to dinner, & dropped him on the living room floor, over cordials, with an audible thud.

In exchange for the other man in the room. Milosz. Her translator's highschool mate from Prague. & lover since age 14. & home away from home. & private reality.

The dinner had been Milosz's idea, to celebrate her first completed translation. He had shopped for it, & cooked it. Goulash with dumplings. In the tin-ceilinged kitchen that is the largest room in the Village garden apartment she still lives in. Which Milosz found for them soon after they arrived in New York. Despite or perhaps because of his baroque English.

She no longer sees Milosz either. He married the woman editor a few weeks after the dinner. When she ceased to be her editor. & divorced her a few months later. Both have been lost in the mist of her past. Only Mandy Murdoch keeps resurfacing. Maybe he thinks that she owes him a replacement, since it was in her house that he got dropped. Or else he's just indiscriminately lonely. She has never been very nice to him. He always manages to annoy her. She hates the way he walks around with a small radio pressed to one side of his head, like a toothache.

He is annoying her again now, on the phone, as he proudly tells her about an article he actually wrote. Last night, or ten years ago. About a Czech playwright he used to know. & drink with. Who became a film maker, in America. A magazine in Prague is interested in publishing his article. How would she like to translate it for him?

She wouldn't.

But ...

No way. She has just started a new translation. —Which is a lie. It's sitting on her kitchen counter, unopened.— She has a deadline to meet.

But this would be into Czech. It would be a cinch for her.

Not necessarily. She finds it hard to translate into a

language she doesn't live in.

But Czech is her mother tongue ...!

Her mother is dead.

Why is she being so difficult. She knows what he means.

No, she doesn't. & neither does he. How many times has *he* switched language realities in his life?

He hasn't. He's no good at languages; he prefers music. That's why he's asking her   begging her to ...

No.

Does he have to get on his knees?

He can stand on his head if he wants to.

He has worked hard on this article. Some of his finest writing ...

If the Czech magazine is really interested, the editor will take care of the translation.

His finest writing at the mercy of a bunch of crumbums ...

Prague is a civilized city, even now.

Of course. Of course. That's not what he meant. But she could do it so beautifully. She knows his style. His subtleties & fine points.

NO!

He doesn't want to argue, but ...

Neither does she. She needs to finish brushing her teeth.

But she doesn't. At least not right away. She continues to sit on her bed, & starts insulting the recradled telephone in effigy of Mandy Murdoch.

You flatulent asshole: she says to the telephone. Du pfürzendes Arschloch. Misérable petit con péteux. Or better: pétard.

Then stops in dismay when she can't think of a worthy insult in Czech. Foul language obviously has no place in her shrinking Czech reality. She certainly never used it at home, in front of her novelist-mother. Or her mother's polyglot father, the old-world corsetier, who managed their household so that her mother could write her novels. Her pristine childhood language contains no word gross enough to do away with Mandy Murdoch. Yet, she turns the grossest Czech into flavorful English, when it comes up for translation.

She doesn't remember talking vulgar Czech in school either. Not even with Milosz. Not even in bed, when they first started sleeping together, still in highschool. Before they left together. & lived together, first outside Vienna, & then outside Paris. & finally in Greenwich Village, in the apartment Milosz found, until the woman editor bore him away on a crest of true Americana.

Leaving Czechoslovakia had been Milosz's plan, with New York as their ultimate goal.

Unexpectedly supported by Milosz's mother, who didn't want to see her son end up on an assembly line. Which was all his mediocre grades prepared him for. That's not what she had ruined her eyes for, to send him to a better school. If her son ended up a mediocrity, he should have no outside circumstances   like his mother   to blame for it. Only himself.

Mediocrity was what he was preparing for, insisting that his girl leave with him. Which was like a convict dragging his ball & chains along after he got released.

One afternoon in July an 'acquaintance' of Milosz's mother picked them up at his mother's house, & deposited them in a reorientation camp outside Vienna. A place that looked like an insect town from a Farside cartoon, where she shared shrill smelly nights with women of different sizes

& ages, & saw Milosz only in the daytime, on endless waiting lines.

Then someone in an office discovered that she could speak fluent German, & she was given an interpreter's job. Which came with a separate bedroom the size of a blister off a corridor wall, where Milosz could sneak in late at night.

He thought they should get married then, so he could share the blister-room officially. But before he had a chance to work on it, a French protestant minister, who worked with an international organization for the resettlement of defectors, put them on a train to Paris.

They shared a third-class compartment with two elderly gentlemen, who addressed them in German as the train pulled out of Vienna, asking: Where they were from? & where they were going? & Why?

Which struck her as none of the gentlemen's business. So she told them in German that: They were newly weds on their honeymoon.

How romantic. & where were they planning to spend it? the gentlemen asked, switching to French.

To test her, she thought, to find out if she understood. So she told them   in fluent French   that she was a lateral descendant of Marie Antoinette, & that they had been invited to stay at the Château de Versailles.

The two gentlemen were getting slightly annoyed with her, & asked in Italian: If they were also planning to visit Italy.

She told them, in fluent Italian, that they certainly were. That they were going to Corsica, to Ajaccio, where her new husband had a distant cousin who was a distant relation of Napoleon's mother Laetitia Ramolino.

The two   now exasperated   gentlemen asked in English if they had distant relations also in England.

To which she replied, in fluent English, that a great-great-great-great-aunt of her new husband had been a secret wife of Sir Francis Drake.

In desperation the two gentlemen switched to Czech. Which she feigned not to understand. Worrying that Milosz   who had been reading a Czech magazine all this time   might look up & say something in Czech. But he didn't. & the two gentlemen launched into an animated conversation they obviously hadn't wanted that 'over-imaginative little parrot' to overhear.

She listened to them severely criticize the organization of the international organization that was transporting them to Paris. & the 'self-serving' French protestant minister who took young defectors into his parish house outside Paris, in a place called Noisy-le-Sec, where he made them work hard for their room & board.

At this point Milosz *did* look up, & threw her a questioning look, but luckily he said nothing.

Eventually the two elderly gentlemen went to the dining car, & she & Milosz found seats in another compartment.

Milosz told her to: Wait! Not always to anticipate the worst. Which only brought it on that much sooner.

But when they were placed in widely separate rooms, on different floors, in the parish house, he became very upset. & protested, in baroque French, that they were married. That their marriage certificate had been lost in the baggage shuffle at the camp. But to no avail.

They were awakened every morning at six, & expected to run errands & do domestic chores, until their papers came through for America. Then someone discovered that she spoke fluent French, & she was placed in the parson's office on the groundfloor, to translate birth certificates, & other proofs of civic existence.

She was paid a little money, which she gave to Milosz to

buy himself an afternoon off from washing sheets, or raking leaves. To take a bus into Paris & sit in a sidewalk café.

Which prompted the minister to ask if it was true that they were married. She said: Yes, they were. She was keeping her maiden name only because it was also her mother's name. & her mother was the well-known Czech novelist Mara Pandora. Maybe he had read her?

He hadn't. & he wouldn't agree to marry them all over again either, as she then suggested. A religious ceremony was no substitute for a legal document.

Besides, they weren't protestants.

She felt that he didn't believe her. Suddenly, her fluency in French gave her a forked tongue. An honest person just wouldn't be speaking a foreign language without an accent, like a native.

At any rate, their sleeping arrangements remained separate. They hardly saw each other. She sometimes wondered if leaving Prague had been such a good idea.

She would never have thought of leaving without Milosz. But when he asked her, she was ready   eager   to go with him.   A] Because she wanted to live with him for the rest of her life,   & B] because she no longer wanted to live under the dual dictatorship of her mother & her grandfather. Who were forcing her to do the opposite of what she felt they expected her to do. Which she often expected of herself also. & might have preferred to do, if they weren't suggesting   insisting   that she do it.

Like going on to a Czech university, for instance. Which the official authorities were also suggesting, in her case. Because of her top grades, & her exceptional command of Russian, for which she received free tuition during her last three years of school. The authorities would have liked to groom her to become an official translator, or interpreter.

It was different for Milosz. He would have had to apply to a technical training school.

As far as she was concerned, her life had not been drastically affected by the events around her. The grandfather complained a lot about the red ink of bureaucracy leaking into his bras, & corselets, & girdles, but he was able to continue to design, make, & sell them as before. —Eventually he stopped complaining, when he launched a season of ink-red bras, corsets, etc., which he called his Hot Line. He'd come upstairs chuckling, every time he sold one.

& her mother felt falsified when her publisher started promoting her as: a subtly political writer, a vital voice in the denunciation of capitalism. But she was able to continue to write & to publish as before.

& both of them were proud of her & of them-selves   when she started receiving her scholarship.

She sometimes thinks that, had she stayed in Prague, she would have written the novel she hasn't been able to write in America. & thought she couldn't write in Prague, under her mother's nose. A novel of revenge, about a fat teenager outwriting her slender novelist-mother.

She's back in the bathroom, finally. —Which badly needs retiling around the faucets above the sink. The building management doesn't lavish maintenance on rent-controlled tenants. She could use a handy man around the house, & should maybe take a break from celibacy. But not with the assistance of Mandy Murdoch. Who isn't handy anyway. Who has only one hand free to do things with; the other is pressing his toothache to his cheek. He's too enamored of his felicitous farts to stoop to practicality.

The gall of that Asshole to ask her to translate for him. She's stupid stupid STUPID to allow him to assume that he can ask her something like that. Is she, too, indiscriminately lonely?

She glares at her forty-two-year old, as-yet-not-made-up mirror face above the sink. She doesn't like what she sees. Gueule de traductrice: she says to her reflection, punctuated by vehement toothbrush strokes: Gullible unpainted translator's mug. Aren't you sick & tired of living in the service entrance to other writers' brains. Standing on tiptoe, respectfully eavesdropping on what is being said inside.

By the Mandy Murdochs of this world. Your novelist-mother, & other self-delusionists.

By the young Czech author, whose 'brilliant' first novel is lying on your kitchen counter, awaiting its transformation into best-selling American English.

They're all less original, in their originals —less witty/terse/lyrical— than what you make of them, you language lackey. After your endless conscientious rewrites. Polishing each banality until it sparkles like Mandy Murdoch's ethnic-sauce-basted chin.

Decreasing your slave wages with every rewrite, you self-defeating perfectionist, with your misplaced pride in finding the *mot juste*. Four cents a word ... that's what they pay you ... oh, how they weigh you ... down ...

Why don't you introduce a little fun into your furrow-browed routine. Turn their deep-thought passages into deep throat. Flatten their jokes. Add necrophilia to their funerals. Slow their suspense to the underwater gropings of algae. Isn't it time you got even with all those authors. For writing when you don't. For which you have no time. Why don't you finally push them off your kitchen counter, & write that novel of revenge.

—Why do you need to write a novel, Mara? Because your mother used to write novels? Your mother is dead. & her novels died with her. No one reads them any more.

Did *you* ever read your mother's novels, Mara? Other than the one you translated? About the young anorexic who knew she would be cured if she cooked & ate her slender mother. While the mother kept cooking 'little temptations', to restore the daughter to former pleasant teenage plumpness.

A neo-Greek tale of mother-daughter warfare in which nobody won. In the end, the two women try to strangle each other in front of a full-length bathroom mirror. The daughter's freshly painted fingernails leaving bloody streaks around the incredulous mother's neck.

You haven't been pleasantly plump in over twenty years, Mara. You needn't keep up the competition. Which you can't win unless you die yourself.

Or do you maybe feel the need to revive your mother's

name   which happens to be your name also   with this obsessive novel of yours?

Which you could start writing this minute. As soon as you finish brushing your dirty teeth. & make up your face. Your mother always said her words came out smoother when she made up her face.

Never mind the young Czech's first brilliance, which you contracted to translate by December 15. Shove it off your counter. Or simply turn it over, & write your own story on the back of it. Then casually hand it in on December 15, instead of the contracted translation. You'd get away with your substitution as long as you keep the title. & the approximate length. —English usually shrinks the original Czech.— Maybe also the first & last couples of pages. No one at your publishers reads Czech. You'd be safe until the pub date. Maybe even afterwards, if your book sells as well in America as his is selling in Czechoslovakia. & Germany. & France.

Unless the brilliant young Czech author reads English. As most brilliant young Czech authors do. & starts reading your translation, for suspected dimming of his brilliance. & starts screaming: Traduttore-Traditore   (because brilliant young Czech authors also know Italian)   across the Atlantic. Into the telephone ear of your dumbfounded editor.

& you'll have a hard time convincing either your dumbfounded editor or the still screaming young Czech that the novel you substituted is better   worthier of continued promotion; of exploiting the 'literary scandal' for further promotion   than the one you didn't translate.

Which you will NEVER be asked to do again.

Instead you'll find a job selling bras, & corselets, & girdles, & control top pantyhose in an intimate lingerie

store that caters to ladies in need of all types of support. &
well-rounded gentlemen.

You're hired the instant you tell the manager that you're
Czech. You needn't even mention your polyglot corsetier
grandfather, whose name the manager recognizes, &
venerates. Unlike yours. Or your novelist-mother's, who
has sunk into oblivion.

He smiles at you, & pinches your butt to check if you're
at least wearing a control top. Before he requests that you
speak English with a heavy Czech accent. Which you don't
have. & hate. Because Czechs have the reputation, in
intimate lingerie circles, of making the best bras, corselets,
etc. in the world. Better than the French.

& you'll hate your carefully made-up mirror face, early
every morning, before you leave for work. Much more than
the still unmade-up translator's mug that is staring back at
you. At ten to noon. Because you can translate at home, at
least. At your own hours. In your bed. In your pajamas, if
you want to, like your dead & forgotten novelist-mother.

Who thought she was doing you a favor when she started
you out as a translator, in America. At the expense of her
anorexic novel, which sold less well, in your translation,
than the Czech original at home. Or the two previous
translations, into French & into Italian. For which you
blamed yourself for years. You'd worked hard at this job,
with novice fervor. You thought it was you, who was doing
the favor, establishing an English readership for your
mother. Whose moon, you thought, was beginning to
wane.

Whose carefully made-up face clouds over hers,
suddenly, in the bathroom mirror. The way her mother
used to look in her forties. A slender dark-eyed
woman with a see-saw limp who spent her life

propped against satin pillows in a wide bed strewn with notes & reference books. A manual typewriter   an Underwood   across satin pajama thighs.

While the   overweight   growing daughter stood on tiptoe outside the sacred bedroom door, waiting to be invited into the temple of maternal creativity. —Of which she, too, was a product. A sibling of many novels & stories.— Eavesdropping on her mother's erratic typing, until she got earaches. A double mastoid every winter, when her classmates got colds.

She'd try to hide a new infection behind homework, until the piercing pain made her fall off the diningroom chair. When her maternal grandfather would come running. & place his old cold hands under her armpits, & drag her to her bed. Exuding a cloud of *Monsieur* by Rochas, from the effort of pulling her heavier & heavier body. The smell lingered in her nostrils after he hurried out to the kitchen, to heat up small bags stuffed with dried camomile flowers, to put over her ears.

Soon after, the typing would stop in the sacred bedroom, & her mother would see-saw in. & hover over her with compresses. & attack her ear with drops of peroxide, that felt cold, & hissed when it touched the heat of her pain.

& she'd feel totally helpless. & useless. At her mother's mercy. A baby again. Horizontal again. & close her eyes against the hovering tower of her mother. Who was drawing up a chair to read her baby-again to sleep.

Keeping sleep away, as she lay listening with aching ears.

She hasn't had an earache since she left Prague with Milosz.

The made-up mother face smirks & bops above the sink,

at the mention of the name. Milosz became the cause of all her mother's disapprovals, from the day she brought him home. When she & Milosz started going steady in highschool. Her mother hated him, even after she told her that Milosz was born on the same day as Monsieur le grandpère, on July 31. Since her mother believed in astrology.

The Squirrel: her mother used to call him. With a smirk: What a nervous boy. Always darting somewhere. & chewing. How could she kiss a mouth full of such small pointed teeth.

Milosz's greatest sin, however, was something else entirely. Something her mother carefully avoided mentioning, & denied vehemently when she finally confronted her with it. Milosz's mother was one of the rotund women who sewed the grandfather's bras & corselets, etc., in the forbidden room behind his store.

What on earth was she talking about! Her mother was no snob. But she was a pretty good judge of character, as a writer. She could smell a rotten egg a mile away.

Her absurd attraction was obviously based on The Squirrel's mediocrity. Which allowed her to feel superior. For which a word of warning: You go shopping for a slave, & you buy yourself a master ...

But her mother *was* a snob. She'd find the absurdest proofs for her innate aristocracy. Like the length & narrowness of her 'good' foot, for instance, compared to the short stubby feet of her daughter. Who had the same feet as the dead father. Who used to worship the mother's feet, urging her to let him paint her toe nails, which wasn't done in those days, when her mother was a bride.

She started losing weight when she lost her virginity. When she started thinking of sex as the weight watchers' exercise. She was feeling much better about herself. Desirable for the first time in her conscious life. No longer the clumsy appendage of a slender mother. Who 'always knew that teenage plumpness was only a puppy-fat phase.'

Which used to enrage her. Hot-eyed with loathing she'd glare at her mother across the dinnertable, desperately turning down all her favorite foods. While her mother berated her for disappointing that dear old grandfather who liked to prepare special treats for 'his two special ladies'.

The Squirrel was gnawing the flesh off her bones. & when he had gnawed enough he'd drop her for another nut: was her mother's smirked prediction.

Which took many years & miles of land & water to come true.

Perhaps it had been more than a prediction: she suddenly thinks. For the first time; twenty years after the fact. Flooded by a heatwave of long-forgotten loathing. Her mother is dead. Do not speak   or think   ill of the dead.

Perhaps removing Milosz from her life had been her novelist-mother's most ambitious plot: One sunny March afternoon she came home from getting her hair cut, & he & all his things were gone. & the printed announcement of his marriage to the woman editor was stuck to the bathroom mirror. The climax of her mother's inspiration.

Perhaps.

Perhaps her mother made an offer the woman editor could not refuse: To publish her anorexic novel in her daughter's translation, with the understanding that her daughter's lover be removed upon its publication.

—Which gives a sudden explanation to the audible thud with which the woman editor dropped Mandy Murdoch, the evening of their intimate pre-publication celebration.

Marriage gave finality to Milosz's departure. It also sped up his citizenship. He had just become an American citizen, when he called to tell her that he was getting divorced.

& that he had changed his name to Miles.

Miles: she said: That's what lay between them now. Miles & Miles of mistranslations, revamped by women editors.

Beginning with the classic example of the Bible translator who changed 'missing the mark' to 'sinning'.

For a while he kept calling, suggesting that they get back together. That it had taken him all these married months to realize that he had been manipulated. Into leaving her. Now he wanted to come back.

But she felt still too raw. Too betrayed. & he wasn't begging her enough.

Besides, she had just started seeing an Italian mathematician, who became cross-eyed with desire when he looked at her. From under the longest lashes in the world. She had taken the long-lashed mathematician home for the first time   after months of desire staring in bars & restaurants   the night Milosz called, & much of what she said on the telephone was prompted by the gooseflesh of passion that had just come into her life.

It hadn't occurred to her then, as it is suddenly occurring to her now, for the first time: That they might all have been acting out a plot conceived by her novelist-mother.

To whom she didn't mention that Milosz had moved out, when her mother called a few weeks later. To let her know that the grandfather had died. She didn't want to hear her mother say: Aha! What did I tell you!

Her mother was urging her to come 'home', to attend the funeral. At least. She didn't stop urging for several months after that, during almost nightly calls. Complaining that the grandfather's death had left her not only bereft, but also without time to write.   Her mind was unable to hold on to anything beyond the length of a poem. When poetry really wasn't her thing. All she could manage were brief laments: There is freedom in the desert / which the orphan seeks in vain. / Desert freedom, for the orphan / translates only into pain ... —Which she was quoting because of the word 'translates'.— Most of her writing time was spent looking after the grandfather's store.

Such a pleasant, elegant store. Still, in spite of everything. It could provide such a comfortable living for someone. Like her daughter. Who wouldn't have to worry about not knowing anything about lingerie. The grandfather's intimate understanding of the human anatomy made his styles timeless.

Her life could be a lot easier in Prague, in the grandfather's elegant store, than sitting in her New York kitchen doing translations. Perhaps translating was not her thing, after all. Wasn't it frustrating, to be rewording other people's words?

& they were having the most glorious spring in Prague this year. More glorious than any spring her mother could remember. It was a shame her dear grandfather was no longer there to see it. It might have restored his incentive to live. Which he said he had lost, toward the end, when pain became his only occupation.

When he said that he was applying for an exit permit. Which made her mother worry that he was losing his exceptional mind. Until she realized that he was applying for an exit permit from life. The grandfather's mind had stayed sharp to the very end. Which her mother found reassuring for her own mind. As well as for the mind of her daughter ...

She thought she heard the sound of a steel trap being set, to catch a run-away daughter. & turn her into a mother's home companion, with the death of either as the only promise of release.

Her own death, most likely. She used to think that her mother was immortal. Not because of her novels, but because her mother never got earaches, or even a cold. So far as she knew, her mother's limp had not been caused by a bone deficiency, or anything like that, but was the result of an accident.

& one of the forbidden subjects of her childhood. What

she knew about it came from Milosz. Who knew about it
from his mother.

Someone had seen a rat in the sewing room behind the store. Which prompted the grandfather to set steel traps under the four long, floor-to-ceiling windows.

Milosz's mother hadn't seen any rats. & she had no idea which one of the other seamstresses said she had seen them. But they were all scared of those traps. Which looked big enough to catch a tiger, or a wolf.

Milosz's mother thought the old gent was giving in to his paranoia, & set those traps to catch spies from other lingerie designers he always accused of stealing his styles.

Or maybe to catch a husband or a lover of one of his women. About whom he felt extremely protective; not to say possessive. He sometimes acted as if he owned them all. As if the sewing room were some kind of harem. Sometimes the men came to the windows, on evenings their women worked late. In warm weather the windows stood open, & they'd hop in. The old gent didn't like that at all.

Nor did he like it when his son-in-law came down to the sewing room in the evenings, when he was in town, to read stories to the late-working women. But the women liked it. & listening to a story seemed to speed up their sewing, somehow, so he didn't say anything about that.

But maybe his daughter said something about it to him. Maybe his daughter thought her husband was down there, doing more than just read stories. The daughter was pregnant then; close to her term. First-time mothers often suspected their young husbands of running to other women for solace & support.

Milosz's mother seldom worked late. She wasn't there when the pregnant daughter climbed into the room through a window, to check up on the kind of story her husband was reading. & CLANK! she caught her foot in one of those traps.

The women who were there jumped up from their machines, & ran toward her. & the husband ran also. But she had fallen on her immense stomach before they could catch her. & was in labor, with her foot stuck in the trap.

They couldn't get it out. Not even after the doctor arrived, & delivered her.

Finally someone   maybe the husband   called the Fire Department, & two firemen came & pried open the trap. Which had completely crushed her left foot.

To everyone's relief the old gent had the firemen pick up all the traps, & take them away with them. Rats were much less frightening than those ghastly things. Although Milosz's mother still didn't see any around. But she sure thought she smelled one, when the husband took off again two days later, on one of his foreign trips. The one he never came back from.

There still was a dark stain in the wood of the floor under the window where the daughter had given birth. To that girl her son was hanging out with ...

She became obsessed with the stain made by her mother's blood, after Milosz told her what his mother had told him. She needed to see it. To touch it, & smell it, to understand her birth. & her mother's limp.

To do that she needed to be alone in the sewing room. Which meant going there at night. Which meant hiding a flashlight under her pillow, & stealing the grandfather's keys.

For hours she waited on her bed, until she heard her mother's erratic typing, syncopated by the grandfather's snores in his room across the hall. She soundlessly glided down the stairs, entered the store through the inner door that connected it to the upper floor, & unlocked the sewing room.

In the light that filtered in from the street, the covered sewing machines looked like the ghosts of seated busty women. With ghostly arms & hands, which moved when the wind moved the branches outside the long high windows. She beamed her flashlight along the window wall, but could not detect any stain.

Instead, her grandfather detected her. & scared her half to death, when his voice suddenly boomed from the dark in back of her, demanding to know what she was doing   alone   in the middle of the night   in a place she was not supposed to be in. Was she expecting that boyfriend of hers to come hopping in through one of the windows, by any chance?

No, she was not. She was looking for a stain made by her mother's blood. But she couldn't find it.

She asked then if it was true that she had been born on

the sewing room floor, while her mother's left foot was caught in a trap.

He said that: the few things she was not allowed to do   or ask about   had their very good reasons. & that, if she would keep quiet about this nocturnal expedition of hers, so would he. Her mother's accident was never mentioned again.

Her mother's nightly pleas for the daughter's return abruptly ceased, after the astounding announcement that Milosz's mother was taking over the grandfather's store. She had always thought her mother had nothing but contempt for the rotund, gossipy woman. Now she had nothing but praise for 'that warm, friendly person, who obviously recognized a good thing when she saw one. How reassuring to have such a reliable professional presence on the floor below.'

Her mother sounded elated. She was writing again. A new novel; something she'd been incubating for a long time. Her telephone calls decreased to once a week.

On Saturday evenings, usually, just when her daughter was getting ready to go out on a date.

She was going out a lot, after Milosz left. Meeting all kinds of different men. Which she didn't mention to her mother either, for fear of being presented with a parade of squirrels. Or other animals, depicting her taste in lovers.

Her mother did most of the talking anyway. About the new novel she had started. A novella, actually, shorter than her usual breathlengths. Which grew glorious flowers on good days. When words were ready & docile. Eager for her touch on the keyboard. But totally elusive on bad days. Unavailable, no matter how hard she tried to coax them. When all she could write was 'weeds'.

Translating couldn't be that difficult. —Had she signed

the new contract yet, for her next translation?—
Translating was only rewording other people's words, after
all. It didn't involve the imagination.

Gradually the calls dropped to once every two to three
months. Then stopped altogether, & were replaced by
sporadic short letters.

In her first letter, her mother announced that she had
found 'a devoted young man'. Had literally found him. At a
street corner. Shaking with cold. Asking for spare change.
In an educated voice that prompted her mother to inquire:
Why he was panhandling. & he told her that he used to
write. But that everything he wrote always got rejected.
Now he had lost the incentive.

Which had been the dear departed grandfather's words,
toward the end: Mara, I've lost the incentive. Which
prompted her mother to take the young man back to the
house with her.

She was glad she had. Now he was cooking for her. &
cleaning. He even took care of some of the secretarial chores
she'd always hated. Which were the bane of a writer's life.
In exchange for room & board, & help with his writing.

The young man was very serious about his writing. &
quite talented, too. He was still putting too much emphasis
on style, though. She agreed with him that : *Le style c'est
l'homme*. Or *la femme*, as the case might be. But style should
never overshadow content.

Her mother's main talent   including writing   was
pressing people into service: Milosz used to say. With
reciprocated antipathy. Her mother could extract devotion
from a stone.

Perhaps she could. & did. But she rewarded that
devotion. Her mother would leave all her earthly

belongings to the devoted young man, when she died. Almost a year ago.

—Everything, except a large antique mother-of-pearl make-up case 30 inches long, & 16 inches wide, which arrived in the mail a few weeks after her death. With a note inside that read like a message in a fortune cookie: A careful make-up saves face.—

She felt robbed. Betrayed by her mother for letting her think that she would leave everything to her, when she'd urged her to come 'home'. The house. The grandfather's business. Potential royalties from her eleven novels. Her 'siblings'. Instead of giving it all away to a devoted young man she'd found in the street.

Whom she had also appointed her literary executor.

He who waits to inherit a pair of shoes walks barefoot all his life: as her proverb-loving grandfather would doubtlessly have said to her.

Obviously her mother's nightly telephone pleas for her return to Prague had been concerned only with her mother's loneliness, & sudden lack of household service. Not at all with the future & security of her daughter.

Who might risk having her passport taken away, if she returned to her native Czechoslovakia. Where she might be accused of embezzling the money the authorities had spent on her education. Of defrauding her country of the fruits of her education. She might never be able to leave again.

Which she never mentioned to her mother to justify her refusals.

Which her mother would have shrugged out of the way, as: sheer hysteria, since her mother had no experience with

passport offices, & visas, & residence permits, & green
cards, & the eventual haven of citizenship. Or, if she *had*
known about these things, she might have counted on them
to trap the run-away daughter.

Who had overestimated a daughter's importance in a
mother's life. Expecting the mother to remain selflessly
maternal toward a daughter who refused to become
selflessly filial.

Suddenly, one morning, her bottomless self-pity was
replaced by a feeling of release. *For no outward reason: she
was still rewording other writers' words.* Of gratitude toward
her mother, who cut her loose when she cut her off.

Her directions were no longer dictated by her mother:
Away from her mother; in the opposite direction. She was
free to go anywhere, in her own pair of shoes.

Suddenly she no longer needed to go out quite so much.
To meet so many different men.

Most of whom have long since slipped back into
namelessness.

She has been making up a list of them, to amuse herself
between translations. She wants to write brief individual
sketches about them. Their rituals of coming on & bowing
out. A collection of thinly disguised indiscretions, which
she wants to call: MY PAPER HAREM.

Which could become another entertaining substitute for
the young Czech's novel she has just opened on her kitchen
counter. —Although she would have to sacrifice MY PAPER
HAREM, of which she is currently enamored, & change it to:
THE MAN WHO USED TO BE FAT. Which is the literal
translation of the Czech title.

In the already existing French translation it became: A

L'OMBRE D'UN GROS PETIT GARCON (IN THE SHADOW OF A
FAT LITTLE BOY) & in the German: DER DICKE JUNGE
VERFOLGT MICH IMMER NOCH (THE FAT BOY TRAILS ME
STILL).

Maybe she could put the title in the plural: MEN WHO
USED TO BE FAT / IN THE SHADOW OF FAT LITTLE BOYS /
FAT BOYS ON MY TAIL. (The word 'tail' in his title would
please the young Czech author, she feels.) & get away with
slipping her own fairytale between the unsuspecting covers.

The young Czech's novel is brilliantly short. 143 pages,
some of them mere paragraphs; in fairly large type.
Approximately 38,400 words. $1,536 at four cents a word.
Less than minimum wages ... unless she turns in her first
draft.

Which she normally does very quickly, directly into the
typewriter, reading the book as she types along. Except for
technical subjects, when a character works on the railroad,
or is a brain surgeon, or a spelunker, she rarely needs to
consult a dictionary.

Which must be how other translators make their living.
Instead of rewriting endlessly, as she does, losing all
self-respect in her respect for the author.

—Translators who translate into their so-called mother
tongue, in which they live their lives. Who have little
intimacy with the language from which they translate.
Which remains 'foreign' to them. Which they know mainly
from reading it. & studying it. Therefore it does not spook
their mother syntax, their homespun idioms, their slang.

Translators who occasionally unwittingly transform: *des
serins sauvages* (wild canaries) into serene savages. Or *am
Weiler vorbei* (past the hamlet) into: a while ago. Or

la goutte militaire (gonorrhea; soldiers' drip) into military gout.

Which few readers notice. Which she probably is the only one to notice. & get upset about.

She became so upset over the footnote 'untranslatable pun' for *Paris sous la pluie, se plairont-ils autant qu'ils se sont plus*, in a film subtitle, that she couldn't rest until she came up with *Paris under the weather, will their next appointment weather disappointment.* Of which she's still proud.

Which she mailed to the subtitler, with a copy of the 'Translator's Credo' she drew up for the occasion: 'Everything that has been expressed in the original can & must be re-expressed in the translation, without loss of meaning or of flavor. The perfect word always lurks in the etymological root canal. It is the translator's obligation to extract it, even if it takes a lifetime.'

She never received an answer.

She wonders how long it took the translators of the French paperback & the German hardcover. Which her editor sent along with the original Czech.

—& a note: 'These ought to be helpful, since you also know French & German. You might like to see how the others handled this young man's much publicized terse staccato style …'

Which she finds insulting. After all the books she has done for him by now. Another stab at her translator creativity. It would serve him right if she handed in an original text of her own, on the day of the deadline.

Which she has never missed yet. She'd better get started if she wants to meet December 15.

Instead she's playing in her PAPER HAREM. Making a list of inmates.

Which forces her to look into the past. Something she has

avoided doing, since Milosz left. But which she needs to do if she wants to write about it.

Writing regurgitates the past; not necessarily your own: her mother liked to tell her interviewers: Half-digested slices of life, that rise in your throat. & give you heartburn.

She wonders how much of her mother's artful heart burns in her books. & how much of her own heart will flare up again, even though she's looking for the funny side in these more or less brief encounters.

In which her heart may not have participated as much as she'd thought at the time. *Or* her mind. She can't have been too aware, or she'd have less trouble remembering who succeeded whom, on the chorus line. Or how they met.

She can't even remember the name of the long-lashed Italian mathematician, who used to give her goose bumps just by staring at her.

With Milosz, sex had been an extension of their finding each other, back in highschool.

By misunderstanding. Someone in their class told Milosz that 'the fat one puts out'. He put a testing arm around her, on their way home from school, & steered her to his house, with calculated inadvertence. Feigning surprise when his mother wasn't there, when they both knew that his mother was at work, in the grandfather's sewing room.

He was too inexperienced to notice that he was deflowering a virgin. & she felt no pain. It was only afterwards, when his informant wanted to know how he'd made out, that he realized that he'd picked the wrong fat one. A much less fat one. Which he felt compelled to tell her. When the only word she heard was 'fat'. The girl who allegedly 'put out' was enormous.

By then they had become inseparable. They thought of

each other as the home they didn't feel they had at home. Bed was a nest in which they snuggled, giggled, & played word games before, after, & sometimes while they made love. They were playmates, more than lovers. They walked around foreign countries holding hands.

With the long-lashed Italian sex was a distinct, separate subject. Which you learned, like driving a car. It required seriousness & concentration. You got better at it with practice. It took you out of yourself, to uncharted space, with implications of the ominous, that gave a razor edge to pleasure.

It was a new experience for her. & for a while it became an obsession. Sex was the background thought behind whatever she was doing. Translating. Shopping. Getting her hair cut. She looked at men, speculating about their talent in bed.

Speaking Italian with him   a language she had learned from her grandfather, but had not lived in before   added a touch of irreality to their trysts. His English was a pain in the ear. At least to her. She had a low tolerance for people who wouldn't   or couldn't   switch to the sound reality of their environment. But he sang like an angel.

Angelo? Had that been his name? Probably not.

He'd sing to her, usually before they made sex. Afterwards he usually called his mother, in Reggio, Calabria. From her phone beside the bed.

After several months of calls she showed him her phone bills. Offending him deeply: She was petty. Jealous of his mother, who was & always would be the foremost woman in his life. His mother enjoyed hearing the voice of her distant son getting ready for sleep, just when she was getting up, in Reggio, Calabria. If she really loved him … If she loved *her* mother …

No gesture of reimbursement. But he had kindled a new need in her, & they made up.

Until the next time, when he called Reggio, Calabria, again while she was in the bathroom. After that she moved the phone to the kitchen, offending him irretrievably.

How can she not remember his name?

She can, of course, invent one for him. Something saintly, or heroic, that would make him feel understood. Francesco   Michele   Garibaldi ...

She'll have to invent different names for all of them anyway, to avoid libel suits if she submits her PAPER HAREM for publication, instead of the young Czech's novel. But what if her invention turns out to be his real name. Which she remembers without remembering. He'll sue the pants off her, the cheap son of a bitch.

She lists him as NUMERO UNO which mirrors his self-image as the sex guru of women in America. Who sigh a collective: AAAAAAAAAHHH, when he enters a room. In anticipation of his teaching: That they have to work for their orgasms.

Which Italian women know from their catechisms. They grow up with the concept of the original sin. They know how to make their sins count before they confess them.

It occurs to her in retrospect that NUMERO UNO was an atheist.

Perversely, #2 surfaces complete: Dr. George Siebert. Department head of Numero Uno. Gangly tweed suit. A rounded forehead, heightened by receding hair. Pale eyes; no lashes. Moist, readily puckering lips. Thin black cigarettes.

She met him in an Italian restaurant on West 26th Street,

during a telephone-bill argument with Numero Uno. Which they continued in English, when Dr. Siebert joined them at their table.

He smiled sympathy at her: Well, my dear. What do you expect. He's a foreigner after all. Or something to that effect. Then cryptically pronounced that: All love was costly. Hardening her conviction that Numero Uno should pay for his mother-loving calls. & Numero Uno's conviction that she would pay for them if she loved him.

It set the stage for their irretrievable break-up a few days later. But when she got home that evening after their Italian dinner, it struck her that Dr. George Siebert was a Machiavellian Prince. No wonder he was a department head. He might be an amusing change after so much serious sex.

The Prince rang her doorbell as soon as Numero Uno told him that: He was through with the cheap bitch who hated his mother. & her own mother, too.

He arrived bearing four roses, wine, & a gourmet take-out dinner for two, without checking first if she was free. Or interested. Or did, maybe, not enjoy eating at home, after translating there all day, at her kitchen counter. She let him in anyway, anticipating an evening of wicked wit.

But Dr. George Siebert was a mono-rail pragmatist. & apparently pressed for time. He ate in rapid silence, & was playing with a box of white-&-green-striped condoms while she prepared to pour them brandy. Feigning fascination she asked him to pull one out, then poured brandy into it. He departed. End of #2.

She sat laughing into her brandy glass after he left. Picturing him badmouthing her to Numero Uno. Whose chances for tenure she had unwittingly increased.

#3: The cartoonist Marino Mons who wanted her to translate *The Diplomat's Daughter Who Slept with Emily Post* into all the languages she knew, for possible syndication.

They were sitting in her kitchen in early winter twilight when he said: O, Mara Pandora, you're becoming more and more beautiful as the light goes down.

She thought he was joking, in keeping with the tone of his cartoon. But when she realized that he wasn't, that he was being seriously romantic, she couldn't resist saying: that she was a real knockout in a blackout.

Spoiling not only his mood but also an amusing, potentially well-paying job.

Numero 4: Maurice. No last name. A grey-curled sailor from Toulon. Short & sweet. Her first one-night stand.

He was touchingly happy that he could speak French with her, in New York City. & wanted her to tell him: I LOVE YOU in all the languages she knew.

He had misty-eyed fantasies about fidelity. & told her that whooping cranes committed suicide after the death of their mate. But her reply that: She'd always known that monogamy was for the birds was lost on him. She couldn't find a French idiom to translate 'for the birds', & was distracted through most of their evening together, trying to find a way to say it.

He gave her the silver saint he carried around his neck.

He also gave her crabs.

#5: Also named Maurice. Maurice Sweeney. A chimney sweep who came to clean out the flue above her fireplace. & stayed a week.

He was nimble as a monkey & hoisted her up with him, to make love to her in blackness.

He made a cult of black, which was the color in which all

colors slept: he said.

& he poured cold water on his thick black hair, then went outside into her little garden in the snow, to let it freeze into a glistening helmet.

You mean that you got to translate every word on all those pages: he said, leafing through the manuscript on her kitchen counter. Leaving soot marks. & laughing.

She spent a translationless week of laughing irreality. That made her feel that she was living a projection of herself into a chimney of pure black glitter.

On a sun-waxed January morning he suggested that they take a ferry ride to Staten Island. It was a day when all things looked larger than their usual size. A few steps outside her apartment she saw a sparrow the size of a pigeon. He hadn't seen it, & laughed, saying: she had big eyes. But then they passed a dog the size of a cow, & he laughed, because the world was growing the size of their love.

On the boat they sat across from a monumental matron with a briefcase who stared her up & down, taking a detailed inventory of her clothes. Which were black, to please her chimney sweep. Black shoes ... black stockings ... tight black pants ... big black jacket ... a huge black ring ... : the monumental matron kept muttering. Right into her face, in Italian. As though she were talking to her.

When they got off her chimney sweep wanted to know what the woman had been saying to her. She was about to translate for him, when a very tall, very black man in a white uniform that looked to her like some foreign army, made a beeline for her through the outpouring crowd, & asked her, in French: If she could put him back on the road to Paradise.

Paradise?

Oui, Madame. He just wanted to go home.

Where was home?

Le Sénégal, Madame.

She didn't know what to tell him, & he sadly walked away.

Her friend, the chimney sweep, wanted to know what that was all about. She translated, & he laughed, saying that the man was some fancy doorman trying to pick her up.

He suggested that she hurry after him, because he, Maurice Sweeney, lived on Staten Island. & needed to go home now, back to his wife & kids. & other ladies' flues that needed cleaning.

The young Czech's novel starts with a photograph the first-person narrator is yanking out of the first page of a bulky blue-velvet album. He holds it in his hand & studies the 'serious baby, still of androgynous age, fiercely staring at a lit-up Xmas tree, with the curiosity of an archaeologist'. Before he tears it up. In the present tense.

She assumes that the reader is being introduced to the future fat boy. & reads on   instead of continuing to translate   because of a similar bulky blue-velvet album in her own Czech childhood.

Her grandfather kept it hidden under the satins, tulles, & elastics that became the intimate lingerie he designed. Which roundish women with tired eyes sewed for him in a long, tin-ceilinged room behind his store. The room hummed & murmured all day long. Sometimes it gurgled, like bottled laughter.

She was not allowed to go inside. & remembers standing in the doorway, a child of four or five, peering at the fine grainy mist that seemed to rise from rows of lamps on sewing machines. While her grandfather went to get the bulky album, to show the documented progress of 'our growing girl' to smiling, nodding customers.

Making her feel like merchandise, another one of her grandfather's intimate creations, as she grew older. & self-conscious.

The first-person narrator studies the serious baby on a later photograph, taken on its first birthday. It is fiercely staring at a single candle lit in the center of a cake. Straining from its seated mother's arms, holding baby fists to baby ears, as if to block out a siren. Or a scream. No trace of a smile.

She rereads the paragraph with a deepening frown. Because of a similar photograph of a grim-faced baby straining from its seated mother in the similar album. Except that she remembers crutches leaning against the seated mother's chair. A wheelchair? Which the young Czech author doesn't mention.

Instead he mentions the baby's father. Who materializes for the narrator with the help of a magnifying glass: Standing behind the mother's chair. A shadow of reassurance.

He dies the next day, under mysterious circumstances. About which the growing boy vainly asks his mother. & also his maternal grandfather, who raises him so that his mother can write novels. But they don't tell him. They tell him instead what a brilliant philologist his father was. How he traveled all over the world, 'collecting sounds'.

Stranger & stranger.

The day his father dies, the serious baby has an earache that develops into mastoiditis, & requires an operation. He is given ether, which prompts his first memory: Of a beautiful clear light that grows & widens all around him into boundless space. & of a beautiful clear sound that lifts him up, & carries him far away.

He later recognizes the sound, or something close to it, when he hears Buddhists chant AUM over the radio, when he is twelve. & getting fat. It is the sound of longing for something far away in a far-away landscape of light. Which he desperately wants to reach. & thinks he is maybe about to reach when he has his first experience of sex with the most beautiful girl in his class, a few years later.

The mastoid operation leaves a deep scar behind his right ear. Which becomes 'his shame', when he starts school. When his grandfather cuts his shoulder-length hair 'to make our boy look like a boy'.

He's first in his class, & always gets to sit in the front. Plagued by fear fantasies of all the others sitting behind him, looking into his brain through the ugly scar. Poking pencils & compass points into it, to get a better look.

He is getting fatter & fatter. Hating himself. & his slender mother. & his slender grandfather. Who smilingly assure him that: It's only puppy fat. That will melt away in no time when he grows up. They, too, had been chubby at his age: they tell him.

There is a photograph of a scowling boy of thirteen. With a dreadful haircut that looks as though he had been shorn for lice. His legs are like tree trunks, sticking out of the short blue pants that constituted the lower half of the school uniform in spring & early summer.

The narrator tears it into unrecognizable pieces. Which he holds in his cupped palm, addressing the torn-up boy in the second person.

I'm sorry you hated them so much: he says: & your fat self even more. But you're skinny now. You haven't been fat in over ten years. & they're dead. Your grandfather has been dead for a long time. & your mother died just recently. That's why we're here, clearing out her left-overs.

Which are also your left-overs. Throw them out. The liver-spotted mirror in your boyhood bathroom no longer reflects your teeth-clenched grimace, as you scream over the running bathwater: That your mother & your grandfather are responsible for your father's death. If they didn't murder him outright, they drove him to suicide. The evasive sadness that falls over their faces every time you ask about him is nothing but guilt. They plotted to get rid of him, just as they're plotting to get rid of you. & since everything you're thinking these days has sexual motivations, you think that your forever-writing mother & her language addict of a father have a sordid incestuous relationship. & you picture them in anatomically impossible positions of sordidness.

You vow to expose them. The authorities are sure to become suspicious when a second death occurs in their house. Your death. You're going to avenge   & join   your dead father.

Who, in a thought flash, may just have walked out, the day after your first birthday, the day you got your earache, because he couldn't stand those two any longer either. He just quietly disappeared, address unknown.

But you quickly rule that out. Your father wouldn't have left you behind, in the vipers' nest. He would have taken you with him, on his sound-collecting trips all over the world. He *has* to be dead. He is really lying under the tombstone in the cemetery, where your hypocritical mother & grandfather drag you the day after your birthday, every year of your life. & make you place their guilt wreath on his grave. It would serve those two right, if the police caught on to them, after they find you dead, too.

You sneak into your mother's bedroom, the one day in the week that she goes out in the daytime. To lunch with her editor. With whom, you think, she's probably having an affair. Picturing them in anatomically impossible contortions.

You sit down at the foot of her bed, & you stuff her support stocking into your mouth. & hold your nose. You're going to choke to death right on her bed. For her to find her dead fat son as soon as she gets back. Half-drunk, as usual, from her luncheon cinzanos. When she'll start screaming for her father who'll come running on his brittle old legs.

Your heart feels like bursting. All your blood is in your head. You see your eyes bulge, & your face turn blue, in your mother's full-length mirror. —In which she watches herself write, you think.— Your fingers let go of your nose. Your hands fly to your mouth & yank the disgusting saliva-coated stocking from your throat. You just sit there, looking at yourself gagging & drooling. & sobbing. Then you teeter to your feet, & watch yourself masturbate.

That poor fat boy is as dead as they are. He'd better be.

The first-person narrator finds a narrow red lighter in one of his pockets & sets fire to the torn-up boy in an ashtray.

Which cracks into two neat halves.

Her eyes have been widening & blurring. She can't believe what she is reading. Which reads like the fictionalized autobiography she has been promising herself to write. To avenge the matricidal anorexic; & other fictionalized daughters she suspects of being victimized in her mother's other   (ten?)   novels. Which she has not read.

How did this young Czech author   this brandnew best-selling literary discovery   get hold of her childhood?

Unless all Czech childhoods resemble each other. At least at the time in which the novel is set. Which happens to coincide with *her* childhood. Which began forty-two years ago. She   & the first-person narrator   were nine when the communists took over.

Perhaps all Czech families of forty-two years ago kept bulky blue-velvet albums, filled with the progress of their growing children. But had all these children been only children? Of dead sound-collecting fathers? & widowed novelist-mothers with leg impairments, who wore one support stocking? & did all these only children need operations on their middle ears, before they grew into fat, self-loathing teenagers, of either sex?

Reading about herself changed into a fat boy is rekindling ugly feelings. Even if she concentrates on the discrepancies, other than the sex change. They annoy her, as if the author were telling her deliberate lies.

Of which she starts accusing him, in her head.

To begin with: She was raised in the belief that her father died of typhoid fever, during one of his sound-collecting journeys. To Turkey, she believes. & not one day, but several months after her   equally documented   first birthday.

As a miserably chubby teenager she, too, often thought that her father was perhaps not dead. That he had walked out on the 'perfect union' her mother always claimed they'd had. So perfect, her father insisted on naming the baby Mara Pandora. So he could have another one, just like the first.

One day he had closed the door behind him forever, because her mother & her grandfather were corrupting his sound collections with the incessant ratatat of typewritten words & shouted foreign languages.

Sacrificing his one-year-old daughter.

Whom he had never wanted to be another Mara Pandora. He'd given in to his ego-maniacal wife, who couldn't get enough of herself. & wanted another one just like herself. A baby-novelist. Before she felt threatened in her uniqueness by a daughter who threatened to write. Whom she quickly made into a translator, before she got a chance to write words of her own.

But never   at any time   did she think that her mother & her grandfather had conspired to kill her father. Or driven him to suicide, in order to crawl into bed together. Their chaste impeccability was the basic myth on which they raised her. They self-sacrificed to the degree of sainthood. Only *she* was selfish. & unreasonable. & fat.

There came the day of disbelief. A gorgeous spring day, when she was fifteen, & had skipped school. Something she could easily do, because she was the best in her class, & always had the excuse of an earache. She was standing in front of a store window, checking out dresses she felt too fat to wear, when she saw her mother & a man walk past behind her, reflected in the glass.

Her mother's arm was looped through the arm of the man. Who was not her mother's editor, but someone she had never met. They were arguing, & her mother did not see her.

She stared after them shocked into immobility. Then decided to follow them, at a block's distance. She saw them enter a hotel. She saw a receptionist hand the man a key, with a routine smile of familiarity.

There was a second door next to the awning, marked: SERVICE ENTRANCE. Which stood open. She threw herself inside & raced up the service stairs. Listening to the sound of the elevator that was slowly rising on the other side of the wall. —With her operated 'antenna' ear, which heard everything better than her 'good' ear; than normal ears.—

She heard the elevator stop on the fourth floor. She pushed a heavy steel door onto a carpeted landing. She saw a door close toward the end of the hall, & crept up to it. Just in time to hear her mother say: You don't have to make love to me. I just want you to understand me.

& his reply: You don't like my understanding of you, Mara. You won't like to hear that I understand your need to be a femme fatale to counter-balance your limp. Which never bothered me, believe me. Not in public, & not in bed either. What bothers me is all this secrecy & drama. This ridiculous hotel room. We're both adults, good God. We're both free agents. I'm sick & tired of co-starring in this passion play of yours. I find it exhausting.

His footsteps were approaching the door. She raced back to the service stairs. & down into the street.

For twenty minutes or more she sat on a fire hydrant, in the sunshine, until her breath slowed down, & she was able to believe what she had seen & heard.

At dinner that evening her mother's face was a heroic mask. Her grandfather was serving *Natilla*, a Spanish cream that was her mother's   & her   favorite dessert. & fattening. She cheerfully refused her share. Smiling: That she needed no consolation cream.

She felt triumphant when her mother's heroic eyes traveled to her face & lingered on it probingly. Until she drove the eyes away with the sickly sweet smile she had seen women rivals smile at each other in movies.

She was shocked when the man appeared for dinner a week later. Introduced by her mother as: an old friend, a painter who had arrived in Prague that morning to supervise the hanging of a show he was having at a gallery.

She didn't say: That's strange. I saw you with him a week ago. While she wondered if writing novels turned people into liars.

Then something strange started to happen. The old friend was sitting across from her, elbow to elbow with her mother. The grandfather was at the head of the table, in his usual 'moderator's' chair, as he called it.

Her mother was talking about colors versus words. How colors seemed to know where they belonged, in his paintings. Did he feel that they guided his brush to where they needed to go? Whereas words had to be whipped into place.

He smiled. Saying that her mother was flattering his craft. With her assumption of ease. Of grace. Colors, too, needed to be coaxed   mixed & remixed   painted over. Readers of her mother's novels certainly didn't feel a whip behind her eloquent prose ...

She was looking at him. Thinking: He's nice. I like him. Too bad he has to be mother's lover ... When his warmly smiling, likable face began to bloat. & turn a repulsive greenish-purplish-grey. A repulsive balloon, which gave off a stench. Like farted cabbage.

Then, just as suddenly, his face was its normal size & color again, likable & smiling.

She sat through dinner with averted eyes & pinched nostrils. As soon as she politely could, she escaped to her room, pretexting homework.

She told no one what she had seen, not even Milosz, & had almost forgotten about it, when her mother received the news that her friend   the painter whose show was opening that very evening; who'd just eaten dinner with them   had mysteriously drowned in the bathtub of his hotel room.

She wondered if it was the same hotel room she'd sneaked up to. & if it had been his drowning face that had disgusted her so suddenly at the dinner table.

She ran over to Milosz's house to tell him, although it was almost dinner time, & being late for dinner, or not showing up at all, was a sin the grandfather did not readily forgive. Also, Milosz's mother would probably be there, but she had to tell someone, & Milosz was the only one who, she thought, would take her seriously.

He did. & said that, if she felt so disgusted, it must have been the painter's refusal to die that she had seen, not his death itself. Because death was something beautiful. Glorious & aromatic, not repulsive at all.

Irritating his mother, who overheard their conversation. & felt criticized by her son's stupid death wish. In her performance as a mother, for which she accepted nothing but applause. Sewing her once-beautiful eyes out to send him to a better school. Where he was learning nothing, obviously, unlike that girl of his, who was learning plenty. For free. He was a self-romantic imbecile, who glorified death because he still believed in his teenage immortality.

Then she sat her down, & questioned her about what exactly she had seen. & smelled. & how she'd felt about it. Had it started abruptly? How long had it lasted?

Punctuating her answers with nods, & ahas. Before she said: She might have known. The old gent's wife   her grandmother   had also been able to read death in people's faces. & all kinds of other things besides death. Bad things, usually. Which was why the old gent had gotten rid of her, after she saw their daughter's accident, over twenty years before it actually happened, when their daughter had just been born.

Or maybe her grandmother hadn't wanted to stick around & watch it all come true. As it always did. No matter how hard one tried to prevent it. Which only made it happen sooner.

Had anyone told her that her grandmother had moved to Paris, a few months after her daughter's birth. Where she might still be living, making a fortune telling fortunes.

It figured. She'd obviously inherited her grandmother's gift. Which was supposed always to jump one generation. A witch bore a non-witch, who bore a witch, who bore a non-witch, & on & on.

Then Milosz's mother pulled up a chair & sat down directly across from her, asking her to take a close look at her face. Did anything repulse her, in her face?

She shook her head, & Milosz's mother went over to the mirror to put a hat on. Because she had to go out.

The next evening after dinner, after her mother had gone back to write in her bedroom, the grandfather came into the dining room where she was doing her homework. He sat down on the same chair the dead painter had sat on, & asked her to take a close look at his face. Did he look repulsive to her? Was that why she had stopped kissing him goodnight?

She shook her head, but the grandfather insisted that she keep looking at him, until she started to cry. The painter had been the first time something like that had happened to her: she sobbed: & she'd had no idea what it meant until after he drowned.

Her grandfather sighed. & muttered something about psychic women being more concerned about the fate of strangers than about their own flesh and blood.

He was leaning his cheek across the table, demanding that she give him a kiss if he really didn't repulse her. She forced herself to do it, with stiffening lips. He did repulse her. But not the way the painter had repulsed her, suddenly, disgusting her with his suddenly inflated face. Her grandfather repulsed her for himself. & because he prepared the food that made her fat. Which she was trying not to eat any more.

From that day on, until she left Prague with Milosz, her grandfather kept trying to trick her into predicting his death. Cornering her to make her look at him, & tell him 'honestly, to his face': If he should renew his season ticket to the theatre. Or bother to buy a new wintercoat.

A few months before he died —when she was living in New York; still with Milosz— her mother sent a photograph of herself & the grandfather, taken on his seventy-ninth birthday. His face turned into a skull, as she looked at it. & she smelled urine. & dust.

She had no premonition whatsoever before her mother died.

The young Czech's 'novel' does not describe any of this. Nor does his 'fictional' mother have a lover. She merely sleeps with her father, in the sordidly unreliable imagination of the fat boy.

Whose disgusting suicide attempt with his mother's support stocking —If it had been *her* mother's support stocking, the smell of tearose would have made him gag sooner.— sounds like a prank, compared to her own. Which came close to succeeding. & did real damage, unlike the fat boy's.

She stole a bottle of fabric glue from the forbidden room behind the grandfather's store, & glued her lips & nostrils together. She had fainted, & fallen off her bed, by the time the grandfather found her. When he barged into her room, looking for his glue.

Which could be peeled off after soaking it in alcohol.

Some of her skin peeled off with it. The pain jerked her back into consciousness.

She looked hideous for months, & went around lying about how she fell asleep with her face too close to the electric heater in her room. Her skin has remained sensitive around her mouth & nose. In cold weather it still turns red.

There was a photograph the grandfather took soon after the 'regretful incident'. To document the trans- or re-gression of 'our growing girl'. Awkward arms & legs sticking from a short, short-sleeved blue school dress. Her face looking as if she had Down's Syndrome. The memory of it makes her wish for a first-person narrator to tear it up & burn it.

Maybe it *was* her photograph   her whole bulky blue-velvet childhood   that the young Czech author looked at. & tore up.   & burned.

Does it matter that the fat boy's ear was operated when he was one, & hers when she was three? That his scar is behind the right ear, & hers behind the left one?

She wonders if he, too, has an 'antenna ear'. Which hears with almost eery keenness. Much more keenly than the unoperated ear. Sounds have direct access through the deep ugly scar.

Which used to be as blatantly exposed as the fat boy's. Her grandfather, who combed her hair until she was twelve, insisted on piling it into a bun on top of her head, 'to make her look like the little lady she was'.

& her fear fantasies were exactly the same. Not only in school, but also on trains, & buses. In the movies. Wherever someone sat behind her.

What shocks her the most, though, & makes her question the originality of the young Czech's text, is the anaesthesia-induced sensation of expanding space & light. Of being carried to heaven on a beautiful clear sound. Which she, too, remembers with deep longing. Although only since age three.

Which she also tried to duplicate with sex. Although much later than the fat boy. Only after she learned to think of sex as a vehicle, after training with the long-lashed nameless Italian, after Milosz moved out.

She wonders if a female Milosz will soon come into the fat boy's life.

He strikes her as being less smart than she used to be, at his age. & there seems to be less emphasis on languages than during her own fat past.

Her grandfather spoke six languages, not counting Czech. Which he literally force-fed to her, at mealtimes. A different language for each day of the week, with Czech reserved for Sundays. The one day her mother emerged from her writing-bedroom at one p.m., to share the special middle-of-the-day Sunday meal.

Often goulash with dumplings. Which she loved. & hated for making her fatter.

Dessert would be withheld until she pronounced its name correctly in the language *du jour*. Eventually it appeared anyway, borne aloft in outstretched grandfatherly hands, to an accompaniment of the chanted repetition of her unjust dessert's name, broken into memorizable syllables: Ba ... ba   au   rhum   Rasp ... ber ... ry   fool.

When the fat boy's grandfather chants: Mou ... sse   au   cho ... co ... lat, on page 54, she pours herself a Bourbon, & decides to substitute her PAPER HAREM for the translation. Under the title: FAT BOYS ON MY TAIL. Then, when the English-reading young author screams literary scandal across the Atlantic, she'll counter-attack with the theft of her life. She has no reason to translate a book she no longer has a reason to write. She doesn't even think she could write it any better.

There is also something else she can do. Which promises her raging curiosity more immediate satisfaction. She can get the author's phone number from her editor, telling him that she has run across a basic ambiguity that needs clarifying before she can start translating. An ambiguity the French & German translators failed to clarify! & call him up. Preferably in the middle of the night, when he's asleep.

& wakes up defenseless. Or furious.

She studies his face on the German hardcover to see how he might react to a phone call   collect   in the middle of the night. He looks twenty-five, maybe a photogenic thirty. A cat-eyed androgyne on a ladder in a bookstore. With a punk haircut that exposes his right ear. The ear of 'his shame', if he did have the operation he describes. Five small diamonds decorate the ear's outer shell. She assumes that he's gay.

Although: One of her straightest lovers used to decorate his ears. With crosses, & crescents, & serpents. Keith. #14? Possibly. His lithe supple body was covered with colorful serpent tattoos that moved into his movements, complementing them gracefully. He was a professional dancer, & often danced serpent dances in symbolic projection of kundalini.

He lived in her apartment for several months. Cooking vegetarian delicacies for her while she translated. They meditated together by candlelight, at 5 a.m., after they got up. & again at 9 p.m., before they went to bed.

He performed the most exotic sex-love rituals her body had experienced. They came closest to her anaesthesia-longing to be uplifted & transported to higher planes. She was translating better & faster than with other lovers. & disliking it less.

One night, a live black garden snake slithered up her left leg, toward their joined genitalia, seconds before her climax. She screamed. & screamed, accusing him of using her as a prop for his sham transcendence.

He left then. Dejectedly. Carrying the little black snake in one of his silk bandana kerchiefs.

She always seemed to stop short at the threshold of

getting there: he said at the door, with a sad smile.

Perhaps he was right. She misses him sometimes.

She pours herself another Bourbon.

The female counter-part of Milosz has entered the fat boy's tale, on page 56. Her name is Mara.

Another one. Perhaps the name has become fashionable since she left Prague. Or perhaps since her mother died.

Mara III literally claims the fat boy one day, on their way home after school. She plants herself in front of him, & asks: If she may carry his books.

All the boys in his class envy the fat boy. Mara is the girl of their collective lust. She has shiny black hair that hangs to her buttocks, porcelain skin, & huge blue eyes. They even forgive her for having a brain.

The fat boy's mother dislikes Mara from the moment he brings her home. Even after he tells her that they have the same first name. Which may be his mother's reason for disliking her more. The Nightmoth: his mother calls her. & tells him: To watch out. He lacks the fire to make her burn. Sooner or later she'll flutter away.

But she doesn't. At least not then. She's sticking around, annoying his mother. Who doesn't like to see her son losing so much weight. So fast. & warns him: That the nymphomaniacal Nightmoth will be the death of him. She's turning him into an anorexic. Which is supposed to happen only to daughters. She's emasculating him.

He laughs. He's astonished that his mother knows words like: nymphomaniacal & emasculate. He wouldn't if he read her books.

He's weighing himself twice a day on the bathroom scale, & feels elated about every gram he loses.

Until his mother breaks the scale.

Deliberately, he thinks. But he doesn't hate her for it, as

he would have in his recent fat past. His mother & his grandfather have ceased to be the target of his emotions. They've lost their importance, & have turned into a pitiful limping nun, & a brittle old monk, who know little about life outside their cloister walls.

They probably had nothing to do with the mysterious death of his father. Who, they have just told him —during dinner, without his asking— died of a freak accident, when his wife's plugged-in hair dryer fell into his bath.

He believes them. That it was an accident. It was so long ago. Seventeen years. It no longer matters. What matters is that he's finally thin & tall enough to wear one of his father's suits to his graduation. A gorgeous sand-colored silk suit, hand-tailored in Hong Kong.

The no-longer fat boy & his enviable girlfriend both graduate with honors...

Which infuriates her. Absurdly. *She* graduated with honors, but not Milosz, who barely squeezed through. No Czech university would have accepted him, if they had stayed. She always let him copy from her during tests. When they were allowed to sit where they wanted to, in the classroom. When the whole class tried to sit close to her.

& Milosz was popular in school. Everybody liked him. But he was hardly an object of collective lust. The other girls didn't envy her when they saw them together. Nobody envies a fat girl. Even if she wasn't as fat as she felt. But she must have been fat enough for Milosz to mistake her for the other, really fat one, who 'put out'.

Former fat boy & girlfriend do not continue their education in Prague to the disappointment of their widowed mothers, & one polyglot grandfather. The stunning Mara is sent to Paris, to model Czech bras & corselets during an international lingerie fair, & her boyfriend is given permission to escort her for the duration of the showing.

Which strikes her as wishful thinking on the part of the bestselling young author. Who may be dreaming of trips abroad to autograph his books. Unless it has become a lot easier to leave than when she & Milosz got out. When most young Czechs dreamt of going to America. To Chicago, mostly. She wonders if the attraction of freedom has weakened with the weakening dollar.

Former fat boy fortuitously discovers a rich Parisian grandmother. With a town house in Passy, where they're able to stay after the fair is over. The grandmother also happens to be a close friend of Pierre Balmain. Who hires the stunning Mara.

Eventually the now model-slender first-person narrator also lands a modeling job. The model couple move to a charming apartment that overlooks the Seine. They belong to the fashion world's beautiful people. & are careful to keep the faintest of Czech accents when they speak their flawless French.

Which Milosz never learned to speak properly. Not any more than English. Which didn't seem to stand in the way of his finding the best buys in town. The wonderful rent-controlled garden apartment she still lives in.

He used to drive her crazy, interrupting her in mid-sentence to ask what she was saying to someone. Instantly freezing the simplest word on the tip of her tongue.

—She used to wonder how he communicated with the woman editor. If an absence of *mots justes* was perhaps a plus in a marriage. Apparently not.

One night former-fat boy's mother calls to inform him that his dear doting grandfather, who used to cook for him in six languages, has died in his sleep. He expresses sympathy & sorrow, but resists her pleas that he come back for the funeral. His grandfather wouldn't want him to jeopardize his newly found career: he says.

His mother wishes she could be as selfish. She hasn't written a word since the grandfather fell ill. She's glad he's doing so well, in Paris.

He thanks her. He can't complain.

But his mother can. & does. About all the details that have fallen on her shoulders. Of which a normal son would relieve his mother ...

She calls again a few nights later, to tell him that his dear doting grandfather has been buried. —Without the presence of his grandson at the grave. Which surprised quite a few people ...

& again, a few nights later, to complain that she can't find a suitable renter for the grandfather's lingerie store. Which leaves her no time to write. Only poems, which really aren't her thing ...

& again, a few nights later, to say what a pleasant life someone could have, running the grandfather's elegant store. Prague was still a civilized city. They were having the most glorious spring ...

His mother is calling almost nightly. Sometimes coaxing, sometimes threatening to disinherit him.

He tells her she's thinking too much about death.

& he's thinking too much about life: she says: His own. She only hopes he's not planning to make her into a grandmother. On top of everything else.

What on earth is she talking about!

She's talking about a baby. The delirium tremens of matrimony: according to an early feminist. Whom she is quoting. Victoria Woodhall, she believes.

He laughs. A baby is the last thing on his mind.

Good. But his mother bets that the Nightmoth has been thinking about it. He still is with the Nightmoth, isn't he?

He's quite sure Mara hasn't been thinking about having a baby either.

Aha! So he is still with her. As foolish & trusting as ever. How does *he* know what the Nightmoth is thinking. She's a career girl. All career girls want a baby, sooner or later. To prove that they're female. Sooner or later the Nightmoth is bound to flutter off toward a man who looks like a good father. Or a good stud. Which would be just fine with his mother. Just as long as he realizes that she won't be available to raise his little bastard. She has her novels to write, even if her son doesn't read them. —She assumes that the baby would *be* a little bastard? He hasn't married the Nightmoth, has he, by any chance? Without telling his mother.

They haven't thought of getting married. They're happy just the way they are.

His mother is glad to hear it. She wishes she could say as much for herself ...

Mara receives an offer to model clothes in New York. They trade apartments with an American writer who has been invited to teach at the Sorbonne.

The writer's apartment is in Greenwich Village, & it comes with a live-in muse. It has an atmosphere that compels him to write. A thinly disguised autobiography: THE MAN WHO USED TO BE FAT. While Mara supports them both.

His book is to avenge the thinly disguised portrait his

mother painted of a fat adolescent boy who falls prey to a Medusa-faced Moth who suffocates him in her huge black wings. At the end, all that is left of the boy is a small heap of shiny black wing dust.

His mother sent him the story still in manuscript. & he reads it, as she must have known he would. Intrigued by her title: THE FAT BOY'S SOUL. He thinks his mother is asking for his absolution before she submits it to her publisher. In case she exposes him with the universal success she still expects every time she submits a new work.

He doesn't let her know that he received it. Or that he read it. He doesn't feel filialy forgiving. Instead he writes his own version of the growing up fat boy. The boy growing up fat. The fat growing up boy.

The words pour from him, released by the exuberance of revenge. He finishes his book in three weeks, the time it took Oscar Wilde to write DORIAN GRAY. On a bet. But then he spends many slow months translating the Czech original into English. He takes his time, savoring the new sound reality of what strikes him as an opulent, fleshy language. Closer to Czech than the bony elegance of French. He deliberately rewrites his original text to adapt it to the new sound. & feels enriched, amplified, when the change of language prompts not only new images, but also unexpected new thoughts. He is translating himself; he doesn't have to respect the author.

Mara knows the editor of a leading New York fashion magazine. Who knows a senior editor at a New York publishing house. They buy: THE MAN WHO USED TO BE FAT.

The book is about to be released when his mother calls. To inform him that she is dying. Of cancer.

Her voice sounds weak. & far away. It is almost instantly

replaced by the stern voice of a doctor, who tells him the same thing. & makes it sound like an accusation: He is a cancer-causing son!

He holds the receiver away from his ear. Stunned by his mother's timing. Just when his book is coming out!

Is this true? Or is it a desperation attempt to manipulate him into returning to Prague? Where she can hold him hostage. Where she can somehow prevent him from leaving her ever again. & somehow also prevent the publication of his book.

—Of which she somehow, mysteriously, knows. His book of revenge, which offends her as much as her manuscript offended him. —The only one of his mother's books he has read.

Then he thinks that his American publisher will be able to bring him back to New York, to promote his book. He hopes so. Why does the past always seem to stand in the way of the present? Instead of being its support? A ladder to success? He finds it hard to believe that his mother is really dying. As an unhappy fat boy he was sure that she would outlive him. But what if it's true...

The doctor's stern voice is shouting: Hello? Hello? Are you there?

Yes: he says: He'll catch the next plane.

The first-person narrator arrives at his mother's bedside just in time to absolve her wicked portrait of the fat boy. For three days he sits on a chair beside her, holding her grateful hand. Telling her about his beautiful anaesthesia memory of expanding space & light.

On the last page, 143, he is sitting at the diningroom table of his boyhood. Where he used to eat too much. & do his homework. & get his earaches.

Before him lies a bulky blue-velvet album, opened to the first page; lopsided. He pulls out the first photograph that documents his life. & studies the serious face of a baby that is fiercely staring at a lit-up Xmas tree.

She sits stunned. Partly because of the almost-empty Bourbon bottle at her elbow. It was full when she started pouring, on page 54. She's emptying it to refill her glass.

She has no reason to wait for morning, to ask her editor for the phone number of this diamond-studded young man who made her into a fat boy. She was smarter than his fat boy. & has drunk enough courage to win any Battle of the Bulge. She'll call Prague Information, & talk to him this minute.

She goes to her bedroom to get the phone. Calling from her kitchen counter makes her feel more in control.

The phone is ringing when she bends down to unplug it. A very drunken Mandy Murdoch is asking if he's waking her up.

She's working.

Oh good. Can he come over then, & drop off his article? He's sure that, when she reads it ...

She pulls out the plug.

His voice is still on the line when she plugs the phone back in in the kitchen.

What happened? he asks: For a moment he thought they'd been disconnected ...

They have: she says, & hangs up.

It takes a while to get Prague. & an operator who sounds as if she's waking him up.

Caught you snoring, huh? she says in Czech. Endearing herself instantly.

Lady, it's 4 o'clock in the morning.

It's only 10 p.m. in New York City: she says: & isn't he supposed to be awake, on his nightshift?

She feels him thinking: Fuck off, Bitch! & is sorry that she didn't speak English to him. Then she'd be another ugly American. In Czech she has no excuse. Except that speaking it again makes her feel strange. For the last twenty years she has only read it. It feels like opening an old suitcase rattling with mothballs.

But the operator cannot know that. She quickly adds a taste of honey to her estranged voice.

Please: she says cloyingly: I'd like the number of ... & carefully spells out the successful young author's name.

The operator knows how the name is spelled. He has read the book. But he can't give out the number. It has been changed to an unlisted one.

Oh? she says. Wondering if the operator is getting back at her. When suddenly her dead mother's phone number materializes in front of her, on the kitchen counter. Large compelling chalk figures, which erase themselves as she gives them to the operator. Almost mechanically: Then please call this number for me   collect: she says in her cloying honey voice.

Disgruntling him further: Why did you ask for it if you had it all along? he says gruffly: Are you testing me, or something. I'm wide awake, I assure you.

Glad to hear it: she says: Then you can listen in. You might hear an interesting thing or two about the author whose name you know to spell.

Her voice sounds worldly, but her heart is racing as a million speculations rush through her head. If this young author has her dead mother's phone number, does that mean that he also lives in her dead mother's house? Which she left to him? Along with all her other belongings, except for her make-up case? Is he the promising young panhandler her mother picked herself off the street? Or is the number just coincidence? Another experience of precognition, triggered perhaps by speaking Czech again? Too much of a coincidence?

The operator's disgruntled voice is asking: If she's trying to make him lose his job? What's with you, Lady? he says: Just let me ring him, & see if he'll accept your call. In the middle of the night. What's your name?

No name. Just say his American translator needs to clarify a few ambiguities.

Huh?

His American translator ... needs to ask a few questions.

Okay.

Her dead mother's phone rings nine times before a sleepy male voice says: Hello? ... What? ... Who? ... Yes, he'll accept his American translator's call.

Go ahead: says the operator.

Hello: she says.

Yes, what can he do for her? He sounds polite. A lighter clicks. He's having a cigarette to wake himself up. She lights one, too.

She needs to clarify a few things before she tackles the translation of his book: she says: But first she wants him to know how much she likes his style. He is a pleasure to read.

His voice brightens. Style is important to him. He thinks

it should mirror the story. Also typographically..

It works beautifully: she says: She likes his style all the way. Those five small diamonds he's wearing on his right ear, on the cover of the German edition ...

He's starting to purr. They're a present he gave himself when he sold the book.

Wonderful. Does he take them off when he goes to bed?

Huh?

She realizes, it's a terribly personal question. But the more a translator knows about the author, the better she can do justice to his style.

He's laughing. She has flattered him. It depends: he says: If he has company in bed he keeps them on.

Is he wearing them now?

No, he was sleeping single when she woke him up. The diamonds are sitting in his bathroom, on a triangular shelf he has to the right of the sink. At elbow height.

So he *is* living in her dead mother's house. She doesn't tell him that she knows the shelf. Her mother used to keep her rings on it, in an abalone shell.

—Her mother never wore rings or her support stocking when she wrote. She wanted nothing on her body that might inhibit the flow of words.—

Don't the diamonds irritate the scar behind his ear when he sleeps with them on? she asks.

Again knowingly. She has tried to wear earrings —on the lobes, not on the shell. They pull at the scar tissue; after a while the whole left side of her face feels like Mandy Murdoch's radio.

Oh ... But .... He has no scar. Behind either ear. That scar is pure fiction.

It sounds so real. Those fear fantasies ...

Yes. Well. Writing regurgitates a collective past. Not necessarily one's own ...

Yes: she says: Half-digested slices of life. That rise in the throat. & give one heartburn.

Ah! She has read his interviews. His voice is joyous now. She has really done her homework. He's sure she'll do a superb job on the translation.

She hates to disappoint him: she says: She was quoting Mara Pandora.

Oh. His joy shrinks, but he maintains his poise. She was his teacher: he says, turning reverential. Or faking it. She appointed him her literary executor.

Is that why he feels entitled to execute her?

He begs her pardon. What is that supposed to mean?

It means that his novel is not as original as his publishers have been misled to believe.

What on earth is she talking about? At 4:30 in the morning!

She's talking about the manuscript of a novel Mara Pandora wrote, but never published: she says. Riding her hunch. Bluffing. A novella, actually, compared to Mara Pandora's usual length. Which he very neatly lifted, & published as his own original work. After performing a sex change on the heroine. Plus a few other minor changes, like the narrator's return to his mother's deathbed. & the circular, happier ending. Improving on Mara Pandora's style, she readily concedes. But considering how Mara Pandora felt about the unimportance of style, doesn't he think she'd be suing him for plagiarism, if she were still alive.

She'd have no grounds to sue him. He stole nothing from anybody, dead *or* alive. He knows of no such manuscript. His book is his own original creation.

There is a silence. Another click of his lighter. Four

clicks. A long intake of breath. She thinks she feels him steady his voice, before he says: If she's maybe had one too many, to come up with a fantasy like that. At a quarter to 5 in the morning. He bets she'd be hard put to prove that his book plagiarizes anything Mara Pandora wrote.

How much?

How much what?

How much is he betting? All his advances & royalties, past, present, & future.

—She's thinking that, whether or not there ever was an unpublished manuscript, she'll be able to write one that would convince any editor that this young man plagiarized the dead novelist who appointed him her literary executor.—

Listen: he says: If this is some kind of joke, it's in lousy taste. In the middle of the night. He thinks he'll hang up now. & in the morning he'll call his New York publisher & ask for a different translator.

You do that: she says cheerfully: & by the time you do, your New York publisher will be looking at a xerox copy of Mara Pandora's unpublished manuscript on his desk. While other xerox copies will be on their way to your other publishers in Paris, & Frankfurt, by registered mail, return receipt requested. With a synopsis of Mara Pandora's story about the fat girl with the shameful scar behind one ear, in all respective languages. Good night.

Now he wants her to: Wait a minute. Hold on, hold on. How did she get hold of an unpublished manuscript by Mara Pandora? Mara Pandora turned all her stuff over to him, when she appointed him her literary executor.

Perhaps. But she mailed a copy of this particular unpublished novella to her daughter in America. For safekeeping. Mara Pandora always worried about un-published work burning up, in case she had a fire in her house. She was quite paranoid that way. —Maybe she also knew him better than he thought.

She never gave him that story, if she really wrote one like that. & if she had written it, how could she mail it to her daughter? It would have caused nothing but pain to the daughter.

... To think that just that morning he put fresh flowers on her grave ...

He's making her laugh. Didn't most writers consider their work more important than the feelings of others. Maybe Mara Pandora didn't expect her daughter to read the manuscript. Unlike his first-person narrator.

He's not laughing with her. He's ranting: What a mean old witch. After all the years of slavery she squeezed out of him. Years of cleaning. & cooking for her. & listening to her hold forth about 'good writing', every night when she got sloshed. When she'd take her famous 'drunken notes for sober tomorrows'.

He broke all her rules when he wrote his book. It made him feel really good. Besides, his fat boy is much more lovable & forgiving than all the daughters she crucified in her work. Her novels have no redemption.

What an embittered old woman she was. He sometimes thinks that it was her limp that wrote her books. Like Ignatius de Loyola, after a canonball mangled his legs. Without her 'flaw', as she called it, she might not have written at all.

He might be right. Perhaps her mother's limp was behind all the things she did. To herself & to those around her. One of her mother's lovers used to say that her limp made her play the femme fatale. He was a nice man, that lover. A painter who died in a bathtub, like the father of his fat boy. Had her mother told him about that?

What? What is she saying?

She's saying that he is speaking to the daughter of Mara Pandora.

Oh no.

Oh yes.

The other Mara Pandora? Who went to America to self-destruct?

The very one. She self-destructed into a translator.

Oh no! & *she* is the American translator of his book?

Of *the* book. Which is *not* his book.

It *is* his book! But ... okay ... What does she want from him?

She wants him to release a confession to the press in all the countries that have published the book so far, declaring that THE MAN WHO USED TO BE FAT is not an original novel, but ...

But it *is* original. It's certainly not in Mara Pandora's style. Or lack thereof. Everything has been said before. Style is a writer's only excuse for saying everything again. Better.

... declaring that the book is not an original novel, but an adaptation of an unpublished manuscript by the recently deceased writer Mara Pandora.

Why? What does she need to avenge her mother for? After her mother destroyed her, in so many of her novels. Which all feature unsympathetic, miserable daughters. —Does she know what one reviewer said: We are told that Mara Pandora has a daughter. We feel sorry for the daughter. —Does she even like her mother?

She's trying to like her, now that she's dead.

Precisely. What does her dead mother have to gain from his public embarrassment! Isn't it better to let sleeping bitches lie ... in their freshly flowered graves. & to think of him as a friend. They should be allies, not enemies. He'll gladly let her share in the book's success. He'll gladly sign half of his American royalties over to her. After she does the translation. She'll be rich when her translation becomes a bestseller.

If: she says.

It will. It will. His publisher will bring him over to promote the book. He'll promote her.

As his self-destructed translator? She isn't sure she wants to translate this theft of his. Which is depriving her of writing her revenge for the fat girl's tale. Incidentally, in case he doesn't know, the title of her mother's unpublished novella is: HER SOUL STAYED FAT. Pretty gruesome, doesn't he think?

Okay. Okay. He'll buy that manuscript from her. For half of what he's made on the book so far. Plus half the royalties from her translation. He'll give her anything she wants just to have peace of mind.

His diamond ear clips?

Sure. Why not. It's settled then? She'll do the translation, & forget about that manuscript?

She needs to think.

He wants her to think of THE MAN WHO USED TO BE FAT as *their* book. He's not a thief. He's a redeemer of literary child abuse. —Maybe they should collaborate on a biography of her mother?

She doesn't answer. She's thinking: That she'll have to crucify herself to fake her mother's manuscript. In her mother's style. Which she doesn't particularly care for, from the little she has read of her.

She's thinking: Where she can find an old Underwood manual, like her mother's. She could probably get hold of some wordprocessing program with a Czech keyboard, but it would never duplicate the uneven look of an old manual.

She's thinking: That she may never have to translate another novel, if she can pull this thing off.

Hello?

Yes?

Are they friends then? A working team? Will she do the translation?

She doesn't know. She needs to think. Maybe, if he lets her change his fat boy back to a girl. & make her smarter than her boyfriend ...

She has trouble falling asleep after her phone call. It's just past midnight after all, even if her voice was heard in Prague between 4 & 5 in the morning.

Preventing her dead mother's plagiarist from going back to sleep, she hopes.

She's lying on her back, staring at the ceiling, in the muted half-light of the street lamp outside. She pictures him lying in a similar position, as he worries about the American translation of his book.

—Which may very well *be* his book, pieced together from things her mother told him. Plus the ugly blue-velvet album she probably showed to him. Before he inherited it. If she were nice, she'd go ahead & translate it, & leave him to his success. But why should she be nice? Maybe rewalders of other writers' words can't afford to be nice. Generous. Only creativity is generous.

Her dead mother's plagiarist sounded generous, on the phone. Willing to let her share in his new-found diamond mines. Does that make him the creator of her stolen life? More likely his generosity was prompted by fear. Lion gestures prompted by rabbit emotions.

In whose bed should she picture him? In whose room? The grandfather's across the hall, where her mother led him the winter day/evening/night she picked him off the street. Telling him that the grandfather, too, said he'd lost the incentive, before he died in the enormous four-poster bed, with the yellow satin roof. Rather than lead him to the abandoned girlhood room of the run-away daughter. Whose celibate cot with the garish quilt might have looked like a medieval torture bed to him. Where unsuspecting sleepers were stretched or shortened to suit her mother's requirements for size. Adjacent too close to her mother's sacred bedroom. To her creative writing bed that slept six dictionaries.

Which he took over as soon as he buried her mother.

Which he had perhaps visited during her mother's lifetime. Kicking the dictionaries to the floor.

No: Stacking them neatly at the foot of the bed. Or all around them: A wall of words.

Because he's not gay, after all. Or is flexible. Sensitive to the side on which his bread has recently been buttered. Or maybe accommodating. Compassionate. Genuinely generous. & creative, in her mother's bed.

Where he remodeled the crucified run-away daughter into a prodigal son.

She can't decide where to picture him, in these rooms she knew so well. & hasn't thought about in years.

Which he has done over, perhaps, & made unrecognizable. Glamorized, to match his earclips.

She makes him get up, & put them on, to reassert his suddenly threatened success. Before she sends him to the unchanged kitchen to make himself a pot of coffee. She wants him to be wide awake, to worry about what she might or might not do to his brand-new literary reputation.

Which suits the personality of his photograph. Unlike the teeth-chattering panhandler, the accommodating caretaker & all-purpose slave of an aging novelist.

She honestly wishes she didn't have to do this blackmail job on him. & even less on herself. Can we ever hurt another without hurting ourselves? She has no desire to plagiarize her dead mother. To reinvent a torture story to fit the hurtful title that came to her on the phone: HER SOUL STAYED FAT.

She repeats   HER SOUL STAYED FAT   HER SOUL STAYED FAT   HER SOUL STAYED FAT   to the bedroom ceiling like an incantation.

She hasn't been fat in twenty to twenty-five years. & even when she felt fat, she was allegedly only pleasantly plump. But fat enough for Milosz to mistake her for the truly fat one. Obesity hasn't stood in her way of attracting lovers. —Overweight would be her mother's thin-lipped word.—   Still, she hasn't held on to any lover, since Milosz, who knew her 'when', for fear of anyone discovering the little fat girl that still lives way at the bottom of her soul. Exposed through the scar behind her left ear.

How can she afford to write this exercise in self-abasement?

How can she afford not to write it? It's her ticket to freedom from a life of translating.

She rolls over onto her right side. She places her right hand under her right cheek, the left arm extended along the left thigh, the position recommended for programming your dreams. She wants to dream at least the beginning paragraph of her plagiarized blackmail story. In Czech.

She dreams, in English:
I am a dwarf, but my world is far from small. All my women are taller & fatter than normal women. Whatever normal is.

Of course my first duty is to the priestess, who is of normal size, but looks taller & fatter because of her robes.

The priestess turns out to be her mother. Who is telling 'all the people in the market place' that the Divine Establishment was right to chain Prometheus to the Caucasus for all eternity, & have the bald eagle swoop down & peck out his constantly regrowing liver, every night. To punish him for showing men how to make fire & cook each other. Without Prometheus there would have been no Hiroshima, no Nagasaki. No gunpowder. No cannonball, like the one that damaged her left foot, with which she has been warning the world ever since.

Her mother pulls up her priestess robe & displays five brightly burning toes, with firecrackers exploding from the tips. Before she tilts backward, & drops to the ground with an audible thud.

She lies there, looking dead. Her profile sharply outlined against the pale blue horizon. But soon her nose begins to curve toward her chin, & her chin starts growing toward her nose. They come together with a click, & form a handle. By which the dwarf respectfully picks her up & carries her off stage.

She wakes up to roaring applause, which turns out to be the garbage truck outside her bedroom window. It's only 8:30 in the morning, but she jumps into the day, to start hunting for an old Underwood manual.

She finds one at her neighborhood typewriter store, where she goes for refill cartridges & occasional repairs. The owner hauls it out from the bottom of what he calls his 'antique shelf'. He has customers who grow flowers from these old keyboards: he tells her: Daisies & anemones. He's seen some of them. The effect is surreal.

She almost buys it when she realizes that it doesn't have all the Czech accents neatly aligned on the top row. The owner is sorry. They both are.

She starts a telephone campaign to all the typewriter stores in the Czech section of New York, on the Upper East Side. No old manuals with Czech keyboards.

She calls the owner of a Czech restaurant she used to go to.

—With a fleeting resident of her PAPER HAREM, the famed French nutritionist Michel Chou. He wanted to taste the food she grew up on, to understand what she was made of.

Michel Chou liked to say that we became what we ate. To which she liked to reply: *Il ne faut pas manger des poires alors*. (Better stay away from pears. A pear, in French, means not only the fruit, but also a dupe, a fallguy.) He felt that she was mocking his science, & eventually he stayed away.—

The owner urges her to come uptown for lunch. He hasn't seen her in ages. Why doesn't she come & put up a notice next to his cash register. Maybe one of his older customers has an old Czech typewriter sitting around somewhere. You never knew.

She thanks him. Unfortunately she's pressed for time.

In that case, why doesn't she just put the accents in by hand.

Good idea: she says: Thank you. Rather than explain to him that she needs to forge one of her dead mother's manuscripts. & her mother never put accents in by hand. Her fraud wouldn't look authentic.

Does it have to look authentic? How carefully will her dead mother's plagiarist look at the manuscript he generously offered to buy from her, in order to destroy it. For the price of his diamonds, his emblems of success. She'd better find a Czech typewriter.

It occurs to her to phone Mandy Murdoch. Waking him up at ten to noon. If he wants her to translate his article, he has to find her a typewriter that has all the Czech accents: she says to him. Ready to hang up & never speak to him again if he tells her that he won't mind if she puts those flyshits in by hand. But he doesn't. He's thrilled that she wants to do the translation after all. She'll love the piece, he assures her. It's one of his finest. He'll find her a Czech typewriter, if that's what she needs to do it. He'll go looking for one as soon as he throws on some clothes. He sounds happy. Now there's a pear in all its forms. He even looks like one.

Although, who'll be the juicier pear, if he comes up with a Czech keyboard, & she'll have to translate his article.

On top of writing her self-immolation.

It would be simpler to translate her dead mother's plagiarist, as an inner voice keeps urging her to do. Do it,

Mara. Just go ahead & do it. You'll mind it less than lots of other books you've translated. You might actually get a kick out of perfectly mirroring his terse staccato style.

Instead she throws herself upon her American type-writer, & tries to start HER SOUL STAYED FAT.

The daughter —no name— crouches by the window of her room ...

She stops. Czech looks wrong without its accents. She feels alienated from this language in which she has not lived since Milosz left. It reluctantly resurfaced on the phone last night. But not enough to dream in it.

She feels further alienated by trying to write like her mother. Who wouldn't have allowed a nameless character to do things in the present tense. She needs to name the daughter who is to be made into mince meat. Perhaps, if she took her typewriter to bed, & wrote across her outstretched legs. Putting herself in her mother's position. But hers is a heavy office machine, not an old portable.

She gets up & limps around her kitchen. Exaggeratedly: Dip—Rise. Dip—Rise. Wondering suddenly if her mother hurt when she walked. Perhaps even when she didn't walk. When she sat writing in her bed. If pain had been a part of her mother's daily life. Perhaps the peculiar smell in her mother's room   like acetylene, covered over with tea rose   had been the smell of concealed pain, not her mother's 'writing smell', as she used to think of it.

She sits down at her kitchen counter, & starts again, in longhand:

Cornelia crouched by the window of her room like a thirsty houseplant straining toward the rain beyond the glass ...

Cornelia was the name of the anorexic daughter in the novel she translated. The only one of her mother's eleven novels she has read. Her mother might plausibly have used Cornelia again. A kind of code name for a daughter whose real name happened to be also the writing mother's name. If her mother had used Mara, like her plagiarist, the alleged mince meat she was making of the daughter might have felt like self-mincing. She's better off with Cornelia.

Cornelia was only twelve, but her breasts were like those of an eighteen-year-old. She reached into her blouse and unhooked the brassiere her grandfather had given her for her twelfth birthday. He had designed it especially for her, for her precocious breasts, and was deeply disappointed when she told him that it felt uncomfortable. The old gentleman took great pride in the perfect fit of his designs. He tried to reason with her, pointing out that, without the slightly restrictive protection of the garment, her breasts might cause her embarrassment. In her gymnastics class, for instance. Wouldn't she rather feel a little uncomfortable physically, than extremely uncomfortable socially. In support of his argument he quoted an ancient Chinese sage, who said that inhibition was the basis of social freedom.

Perhaps Cornelia was too young to understand what her grandfather was saying. She was only twelve, after all, even if she looked eighteen. 'The Thing' made her look fatter was her stubborn reply.

Overweight had become an obsession with the unfortunate girl. In actuality, she was pleasantly plump, much more pleasing to look at than other twelve-year-olds, who were all knees and elbows ...

YUCK! How can she write this genteel vivisection of the miserable teenager whose fat soul still quivers inside her, at forty-two.

—Yes, Mara, you're forty-two.

She doesn't look forty-two.

What do you think forty-two looks like, Mara? Forty-two looks like you look. The older you get, your age is a surprise only to yourself.

Forty-two. Okay, she's forty-two. & still as vulnerable as during those horror years. She shudders at the vision of herself as fat. It may even be dangerous, if the vision becomes too real. It may make her put on weight.

Like that actor   Richard? Yes, Richard   who lived in her PAPER HAREM for the duration of a play called: THE FAT MAN. He was playing the lead, & when he was cast he used pillows for a stomach. By the time the play finished its run, the fat man's stomach was his own.

She hops down from the stool at the counter & limps around her kitchen some more. See-saw   see-saw ... When had her mother begun to resent the daughter she named after herself, but then handed over to the grandfather to raise, because she needed every moment of her day to write?

Had her mother always written? Or wanted to write? Or had she taken up writing only after the accident, as the one plausible   sedentary   thing left for her to do? After she lost not only her painless mobility, but also her wandering sound-collector husband. To a particularly captivating sound, somewhere in the hinterlands of Turkey?

A wandering sound collector, who was also a wandering alchemist. Theirs had been the perfect union that turned the daily lead of marriage into a golden-curled daughter.

To whom she gave an enormous deep-purple amethyst, set in a wide twenty-two carat gold ring, for her eighth birthday. Saying that: Every eight-year-old girl ought to have such a ring, so that she'd never do anything she didn't really feel like doing, in order to get one.

The ring was so large, it wouldn't even fit her thumbs. It used to sit in its box on her bedside table. Sometimes she'd take it out, & hold it up to the lamp, to project color patterns onto the wall.

She showed it to Milosz the first time they slept together. He liked it, so she gave it to him. —Annoying her mother, who didn't think squirrels wore rings. Especially not such a valuable, expensive ring. He'd probably pawn it, eventually, if he needed money.

He left it behind when he left to marry the woman editor. She found it days later in the bathroom, crowning a bottle of nail polish.

She started wearing it then, to go out on her many dates. It now fits her right index finger. Which it covers almost up to the base of the nail. She still plays at projecting color patterns with it, sometimes, when she sits alone in a bar, under a lamp. Despite her fear fantasy that a robber might not hesitate to cut   or bite   off her finger, if the ring resists his pulling grasp.

She plays with that fantasy, too, sometimes.

An excited Mandy Murdoch is on the phone. He has found her a Czech typewriter. Not an Underwood, an old Smith Corona. But it has all the accents. He hadn't realized Czech had so many accents. It's only forty bucks. He'd love to offer it to her, in exchange for the translation. Unfortunately he hasn't any money. Should he come over then, & pick up $40? Then he'll run back to the store, & get the typewriter for her.

She says: Fine. She's at home. Working.

An hour goes by. Two hours.

Which she spends remotivating her mother's life, while adding weighty motherly sentences to the growing Cornelia.

—Depriving herself of lunch, as Cornelia grows fatter.

Finally he falls into her door, panting. Smelling of sweat, & a night of beers. His radio pressed to one pear cheek.

He had to go home first: he explains: to get his article. So she can read it, & think about putting it into Czech, while he goes to pick up the machine. But he had no money, so he walked.

She hands him $40, plus $2 for carfare. She's eager to get started: she tells him: To see if she can still write in Czech.

He assures her that she can. Beautifully. Nobody could do it better.

She's not so sure. But then, she isn't thinking of his article. She's thinking that, somehow, a Czech typewriter will write her mother's story for her.

He runs out, beaming. Trailed by dribbles of Wagner.

His article is twenty-four pages long, single-spaced. Which means six hundred to seven hundred words per page. She feels like strangling him.

She feels like strangling him again, when he returns, still breathless, bearing his trophy before him. Aloft, in one outstretched hand; not unlike her grandfather used to bear mispronounced desserts to the dining table.

The machine won't work when she sits down to try it. The keys sluggishly rise to mid-air, & refuse to make contact with the paper. Behind her shoulder, a shame-faced Mandy Murdoch looks like *poire au vin*. (A pear in red wine, one of her grandfather's frequent desserts.)

The phone starts ringing in her bedroom. He offers to answer it for her, but she flies past him, as fast as in her highschool days, when she'd fly toward Milosz's expected voice. She knows who's calling. In her head, her dead mother's plagiarist is asking: If she's going to do the translation? Has she started it yet?

Maybe he can get the damn machine to work, if he can bear to put his radio down: she yells to Mandy Murdoch. Who has, however, followed her & is standing in her bedroom door like a question mark. He nods dejectedly, & trundles back to the kitchen.

Hello? she says, & listens to her dead mother's plagiarist repeat the two questions she already heard him ask in her head.

She's still thinking.

Still? What more has she to think about? Hasn't he promised her half of his American royalties? Plus half of all the rest? —Plus ... he went shopping for five new diamond ear clips that morning. The same as his. In exchange for that manuscript she's blackmailing him with. She can choose. Which set does she want, his, or the new ones?

She wants his.

Okay. He'll bring them then, when *their* publisher brings him to New York. Unless she wants them sooner. He'll be glad to mail them to her. To show her that he trusts her. To send him her mother's manuscript when she gets them. Or else, he'll pick it up when he gets to New York. That's how much *he* trusts *her*.

She thanks him. She'd love to have them sooner. But isn't it illegal to mail valuables out of Czechoslovakia?

Not the way he'll mail them. She'll see. She'll be quite surprised. He still has her address from when he mailed her her mother's make-up case. If she's still living in the same place?

She sure is. She wouldn't think of moving, even if the building management would like her to.

Why would they? Is she behind on her rent? Is she making too much noise?

She's rent-controlled. They think of her as money down the drain. As a parasite.

He laughs. He thinks of her as smart.

Maybe she's just been lucky.

—& she's curious. Was: A careful make-up saves face his or her mother's fortune cookie philosophy?

He laughs again. But only briefly, as if sensing a stored-up hurt behind her question. He had nothing to do with that: he swears: That was a Mara Pandora original.

He wants her to: Trust him. Trust him. She really should trust him. He's not the average overnight success. He was homeless, when her mother rescued him. He'll always be grateful to her mother, even if he spoke harshly of her last night. When he'd felt betrayed. Double-crossed. Now he doesn't feel that any more. It was true, her mother *was* paranoid about unpublished manuscripts disappearing. Getting stolen. Burning up. & she probably was embarrassed about being paranoid about it. Too embarrassed to tell him that she was mailing copies to her daughter in America. Which was how she was: Embarrassed about being human.

You learned about humanity, when you were homeless. When you became either petty, or magnanimous. Either, your world shrank to an ego-cocoon, & you clutched at microscopic possessions. Like a button off your coat. Or a half-empty roll of toilet paper you'd pried loose in some public shithouse.

Which you carried around in some plastic bag like an extension of yourself. A boil on your arm. & if anyone made a gesture toward it, you were ready to kill.

Or else, your ego dissolved, & you merged with the cosmos. You understood the interdependence of all beings. You were ready to share whatever came your way.

& that's his pledge to her: He wants to share his success with her. Now, will that   PLEASE!   persuade her to translate *their book*!

She can't resist asking: If he means the book he already shared with her dead mother?

Yes. The very one. & when will she stop whipping a dead horse. A dead mère. & start living forward instead of backward.

Mandy Murdoch is at the bedroom door, mouthing: It ——won't—— work ...

Mechanical trouble: she says into the phone: Her typewriter is on the blink. She needs to get it to the repair shop before closing time, if she is to do *their* translation.

Run: he tells her: Run. He'll catch her later. He's happy she's doing it. He knows she'll do a superb job. Nobody could do it better.

He's sounding like a Czech translation of Mandy Murdoch.

Who hasn't heard her speak Czech since the evening they met. When she was speaking to that guy she was living with. Milcotch ... Mollusk ... whatever his name was. Are they back together then?

His name is Miles now: she says sternly. Without answering his question. She doesn't believe in giving out information about herself, unless she's legally required to do so. She still has an immigrant mentality: as the historian Ephraim Lessing said she had, in her publisher's ante-room, where they met, waiting to collect respective checks. She much more patiently than he, who had flown in from Boston.

He knew of her as a translator, & expressed admiration for her craft. Languages eluded him completely. Then bombarded her with personal questions, which she refused to answer.

He invited her to lunch, & came to nap in her PAPER HAREM, before flying back to Boston. He still calls her when he comes into New York.

She asks Mandy Murdoch to carry the dead typewriter to her neighborhood store. Whose owner raises circumflex eyebrows to heaven, informing her —with a searching look at Mandy Murdoch— that someone has ripped her off. He doesn't even want to know how much she paid for that piece of junk. He can fix it for her. Of course he can. But it will cost her. $200, $250 maybe ...

Maybe he can lift out the accent keys, & exchange them for   #$% &*()?(= in the old Underwood he showed her that morning. Which works to perfection. He never sells a machine that doesn't. Not even to customers who buy them just to grow flowers. It'll take time, though. A week, maybe two ...

She asks him to go ahead. To do whatever he thinks is best.

Mandy Murdoch says: He could use a drink. He's been running around all day.

She says: So could she. But ... she thought he had no money.

That's the sad fact.

She could tell him another sad fact: That he has cost her plenty, in one day. All for his stupid article he can't pay her to translate. —Without mentioning her fraudulent project. Which she feels her mother's plagiarist has been buying, on the phone. She feels no remorse. He has been riding her mother's coat tails to success. Well, maybe so can she. & may it be a joy ride all the way.

Her fraudulence is making her feel creative. Generous. So she tells Mandy Murdoch: To come along. She'll buy him a beer.

Besides, she doesn't necessarily feel like going through the ritual of coming on & bowing out, with some new, interchangeable stranger at a bar.

He manifests pear-shaped gratitude. He even switches off his radio, & puts it away in a pocket.

She steers him to an Italian restaurant two streets from where she lives. It is well known for its gnocchi, & a well-stocked bar.

Where they'll wait to have dinner until a table becomes free in the smoking section: she says to the hostess. Confounding him further. Stocking up on gratitude.

The non-smoking section is empty, except for a family with small children. Mandy Murdoch deplores this scapegoat crusade against the American-Indian herb of peace. That wants to enforce pink lungs, in preparation for the Great Asphyxiation. He's trying to ingratiate himself; she's a dedicated smoker. But she isn't listening. She's watching a bony grey-haired woman who resists being taken home by a slightly younger, fat female companion.

Everyone in the bar is humoring the bony old woman. Who may be a grandmother/mother/aunt/the owner of the place. Or perhaps a former celebrity, a former chorus girl, & not only very drunk, but also very rich.

Her name is Grace.

I love you: she slurs at the bewildered barmaid. Blowing her two-handed slobber kisses. You're beautiful, you know that. You're gorgeous.

Which happens to be true. The barmaid is gorgeous. She resembles the fat boy's girlfriend in her dead mother's plagiarist's story. The third Mara. With cornflower-blue eyes, & shiny black hair. Which she wears in a thick braid slung forward over one shoulder. It is casually unfurling in the cleft of a deep décolleté.

I used to look just like you: Grace tells her: I used to be gorgeous, too. Her bony arms flail about the counter, trying to catch the barmaid's busy hands.

The barmaid stops doing what she is doing to stare into the bony old woman's face. As into a funhouse mirror. What she sees does not look funny to her. You're still beautiful, Grace: she lies to both of them.

Let's go, Grace. Let's go: the fat companion pleads. But

to no avail. Grace is now drinking from a pepper shaker.

There is some whispering, & a bus boy is sent out to get Grace's son.

After a while, a short balding man appears, hailed by Grace as: My son! He's MY SON!

Okay, Ma, let's go.

The fat companion has been working on getting Grace into a jacket that was hanging over the back of her barstool. Now the son catches one of his mother's flailing hands & tries to insert it into a waiting sleeve. A long struggle. The jacket ends up on the floor. The son retrieves it. Brushes it off.

He has caught his mother's other hand, which gradually comes wriggling out of a sleeve. The jacket droops down her side. He tries the first hand again, but she won't let him. She's blowing slobber kisses at the barmaid. The fat companion tries to help. Grace won't let her. With combined effort the son & the fat companion pull the first arm back out from the jacket sleeve. The jacket drops to the floor. The son retrieves it. Brushes it off. Folds it neatly over the proffered arm of the fat companion. He places both hands under his mother's armpits & hoists the gesticulating skeleton from the barstool. Which tilts backward & falls. A waiter comes running & picks it up. The son stands his mother on her feet, & starts pulling her backward toward the door. Her heels are scraping the floor. Her octopus arms are throwing kisses all around. Goodbye. Goodbye. Goodbye.

Goodnight, Gracie.

Well, drunk isn't pretty: she says to Mandy Murdoch.

Who nods. But adds: That it sure feels pretty good sometimes. Then humbly requests another beer.

That was like watching a Beckett play: she says.
Wondering if the two of them belong in the cast. Mandy
Murdoch looks the part. She hopes she doesn't. Not yet.
Not for a long while.

A flat light package with Czech stamps is sitting in her mailbox. She unwraps a black satin bra in a nest of purple tissue paper. It has four lumpy buttons in the back, & one in front between the cups. They turn out to be five diamond earclips, carefully stitched over with black thread.

His camouflage is impressive. Undetectable, unless an inspector has been tipped off & knows what to look for. Something only a gay mind would think up: she thinks. Even if he had the sewing done downstairs, in her dead grandfather's workroom.

Which he probably hadn't. Which might have been risky. An invitation to informers, who are a side effect of tight government control.

Unless success has made him heedless, after having been homeless. But that's not how he sounds on the telephone. He probably did the stitching himself, & is definitely gay.

But there is something else that impresses her. Even more than his devious smuggler's imagination: The bra is a perfect fit, when she tries it on in front of the bathroom mirror. Together with the earclips. It fits as though custom-designed by her anatomically knowing grandfather.

Better, actually. It doesn't feel uncomfortable, like the   pink   bra he made for the top-heavy twelve-year-old.

How did her dead mother's plagiarist get hold of her measurements?

Which may still be in the Book of Records the grandfather kept of every bra, corselet, & girdle he made to order. But she no longer has the measurements of the top-heavy twelve-year-old. & she can't remember if her grandfather made other bras for her, after she started losing weight. After his disappointment with the first one.

Maybe he did, & she left them behind when she & Milosz left Prague. With only one small suitcase, as per strictest instructions from Milosz's mother's acquaintance.

Maybe her dead mother kept these intimate   most likely unwashed   mementos. Which became her props, better to crucify the run-away daughter.

Which she kept unwashed, for a more accurate description of the run-away daughter's teenage slovenliness.

Or washed, on the contrary, describing the black juice that came running out of them. So black, it stained the bathroom sink.

Maybe HER SOUL STAYED FAT had Mara? / Cornelia? wearing a 34-B bra, after she emerged from her puppy-fat phase.

Unless her dead mother's plagiarist arrived at a 34-B by sheer deduction. From all the things her mother told him about the run-away daughter's past.

—Of which the present is the inevitable bio-logical fruit: according to Michel Chou & Ephraim Lessing respectively.

Her bra- & earclip-clad reflection in the bathroom mirror makes her smile, as she brushes her hair up, away from her decorated right ear, & thinks she looks a little like her dead mother's plagiarist on the German hardcover. Maybe she'll get her hair cut for a closer resemblance, for when he comes to New York. Then they can go out together as siblings.

The prospect puts her in a heady mood. She hasn't felt so pleased since the day she first walked into the Village apartment Milosz found for them, & discovered the tiny garden in the back, behind the kitchen, with a Rose of Sharon in purple bloom.

It has been blooming every year, from late June through September. There still are a few purple patches out there, on this Indian-summery second day of October. She can see them from her kitchen window, every time she looks up from translating her dead mother's plagiarist.

Whom she has finally started to translate, propelled by his gift of earclips & bra.

She even finds unexpected pleasure in rewording his words. In between she continues to re-invent her dead mother's alleged story. Adding dejected paragraphs to the weight-gaining Mara/Cornelia. Who is taking the lead from his fat boy. She is plagiarizing her dead mother's plagiarist.

Who may not be her dead mother's plagiarist. Just her dead mother's panhandler. & sole heir.

She's looking up, out the kitchen window, to see her tree shaking under an onslaught of smallish black birds. Starlings? They're all over her garden   the surrounding fences   the surrounding gardens. Frantically chattering. A pulsating   repulsive   black mat. Like a blanket crawling with roaches. Which suddenly lifts into the air, & is gone.

She wonders if she saw real birds, or if this was another one of her foreboding hallucinations. A warning? To stop blackmailing an original writer?

Who calls seconds later, to find out if she received his

package. She's translating him with a gloriously decorated
right ear: she tells him: It makes her slide right into his
style.

His laughter sounds relieved.

He's calling every day, alternating questions —How far
along is she? Has she encountered any language problems
he might help her fix? Does she still like it?— with promises
of what he'll do for her when he comes to New York.
Which is beginning to look pretty certain. Probably around
Xmas, he thinks.

Throwing her into a panic. How is she to meet her
deadline & write her blackmail bluff at the same time. All in
time for December 15, & Xmas respectively. —When the
Czech typewriter hasn't even come back from the
repairshop.

It is finally ready. & it costs $280. Which she tells
Mandy Murdoch, who calls to offer his 'mule service'. To
carry the typewriter from the store to her apartment.

She is wearing her earclips when he arrives. His eyes
zoom in on them & remain riveted.

Are those real? he asks.

Irritating her, as usual.

Does he think a translator isn't entitled to anything real.
Only to imitations, as a reworder of other people's words.

B—But ... those must have cost a fortune!

So.

How did she get them? Did somebody give them to her?

There were people in this world who appreciated the
work of a translator.

But ... So does he! She knows he does. If he had *that* kind
of money ... —Did that Mollusk guy strike it rich? He
always suspected him of being something of a wheeler-

dealer. Not weighted down by moral principles. —They *were* back together then?

There were people in this world including her-self who worked for their living. Maybe he should try that sometime.

He works! She read his article. That was work.

She hasn't read it.

She hasn't ? How come? He gave it to her almost a month ago.

She rarely reads a text before she translates it.

Oh ... ? Well, she has her Czech typewriter now. She can start reading his article. —Which she'll enjoy. It'll be a treat for her, after all that modern & post-modern stuff.— Should he maybe wait while she translates it? He'll just quietly sit on a chair beside her.

She's ready to explode. Who does he think he is! To think he has priority over her paying customers. How long does he think it takes to translate twenty-four single-spaced pages!

He has no idea. A couple of hours. Maybe an afternoon. This should go fast. It's into her mother tongue.

She sticks her tongue out at him. He obviously has no idea of what he's asking her to do for him. For free!

Which has already cost her $280 + $40 + $2 = $322 for the typewriter she needs to do it on. —Not to mention the drinks & dinner she bought him, to thank him for finding that piece of junk.

24 single-spaced pages at 700 words a page. That came to 16,800 words. At 4 cents a word, that came to $672 + $322, that came to $994 he's asking her to do a $1,000 job for free, & then he wants to WAIT for it! It may take her two weeks to translate twenty-four single-spaced pages. Longer even, if he wants them to read like his original.

Of course he wants his article to read like the original.

Some of his finest writing is in those pages. That's why he wants her to do it, rather than entrust it to someone he doesn't know. Who doesn't know where he's coming from.

But she's right. He had no idea. He's sorry. He hadn't realized. He's really sorry. He really hadn't realized. He'll go then, & call her in two weeks. Or maybe she'll call him, if she finishes sooner.

She isn't going to. Not for another three months at least.

Three months!

At least. First she needs to finish the novel she contracted to translate. For the money she lives on. & then there's another project she needs to do. Which has already been paid for. Rather generously, in fact. His article is last on her list.

Would she do it sooner if he *could* pay for it?

Maybe. But since he can't ...

She has translated approximately two-thirds of her stolen, sex-changed life. & is still rather enjoying it, to her surprise. Unlike the increasingly painful crucifixion of Mara/Cornelia. Whose progress is threatening her slender self-image. To defy further danger of resemblance she decides to get her hair cut, to resemble her dead mother's plagiarist (?) instead.

She takes the jacket off the German hardcover, to show his photograph to her hairdresser: She wants something similar. But only on the right side. Her left ear must remain securely hidden. Especially in the back.

The hairdresser protests. He has cut her hair for years. He knows about the scar behind her left ear. How she feels about it. But he isn't going to let her walk around half bald. As though she were pulling out her hair on one side.

He has a client who does that. A sweet, pleasant-looking woman in her early thirties, who keeps pulling out large clumps of her hair. Always on the same side, always in the same four places.

She has tried wearing hard clumsy gloves to keep herself from doing it, but then she finds that her hand has wriggled out of the glove, & is pulling out hair again. She can't stop herself. It's a mania that suddenly came over her when she was twenty-eight. & it's getting worse. & of course it hurts when she does it. She's giving herself headaches.

The hairdresser has tried to cover the naked spots with longer hair from other areas of her head, but that doesn't always stay in place. She's a very unhappy young woman.

Which makes her attack herself all the more ferociously.

The hairdresser has offered to shave her head, & suggested that she buy a wig. But she's afraid to do that, because it won't leave her any hair to pull out.

Now: Does she still want that haircut?

Yes, she does.

No, she does not! Her hairdresser doesn't necessarily believe in symmetry. But he does believe in balance. Without those diamonds even that attractive young man on the book cover would look lopsided.

But she, too, has five diamond earclips! Exactly like those. They were given to her just recently, & she has been wearing them around the house. She still feels self-conscious about wearing them outside. Although, with her hair long on both sides nobody would see them anyway. That's why she wants it cut like his on one side. To force herself to wear them in public. & make them stand out.

When she returns, half-shorn & spiky, at a quarter to 5 in the afternoon, her apartment door won't open when she pushes against it, after turning the key. There is a pressure behind it, that seems to be holding it closed, & she hears the iron rod of the fox lock fall or slide across the inside.

For a moment she stands motionless, wondering how she could have dislodged the rod, when she's sure she didn't lock the fox lock. She's sure she turned on the alarm.

Which she must have set off, trying to get in. Although she doesn't think she has been trying for forty-five seconds, the grace period allowed for entering, & turning it off.

Oh my God! she whispers to herself, & relocks the door before she goes in search of the super, to fix whatever has gone wrong with her lock.

The super is a barrel-shaped old man who seems to spend

his days behind a bottle in the basement apartment next door, in the company of four hairless yapping little dogs, & one stern old cat. She always hates to bother him —she's the last rent-controlled tenant in the building— & chronically overtips.

The howling alarm drives her down the hall, & out into the Indian-summer sunshine. Where she stands, stunned, as the realization that SHE IS BEING ROBBED!!! slowly rises to a conscious level. In retrospect she feels a human presence, the pressure of a body, holding the iron rod across the inside door, as her mind replays her gestures of unlocking & relocking.

The super needs to find a belt, & put on his shoes. Which must be taking fifteen minutes, because the alarm stops howling as they unlock the outer door of her building.

He precedes her down the hall, gallantly insisting that he go first, in case there's danger ahead. That he unlock her apartment door, 'in case there's someone in there'.

Again the door won't open. But his time it is because whoever is or was definitely in there put the chain on.

Which the super uproots from the wall with a thrust of his shoulder. A surprisingly forceful thrust, for a man of his age & alcohol consumption.

The super still in the lead, they cautiously sidle inside. They see no one, only the gaping kitchen window.

& gaping closet doors in her bedroom.

& empty spaces where her wintercoat & leather skirt had hung. —Luckily she's wearing her long leather jacket & leather pants.

The five diamond earclips have disappeared from the ashtray on her bedside table. As has an envelope with quarters for bus fare.

Her mother's make-up case is no longer in the second

dresser drawer. Neither is the large amethyst ring she'd been keeping in it.

Together with her American passport: she thinks. & panics, with her immigrant mentality. Then feels almost grateful to her robber(s), when she finds it in the third drawer, buried under underwear.

She's grateful also that he/they didn't take or destroy her almost finished translation. Which sits untouched in a neat pile on the kitchen counter.

—& gives her an idea that further increases her gratitude to the robber(s). To the point of completely forgiving the loss of her precious earclips. —Just after getting her hair cut, to wear them. Which makes her feel like the O'Henry heroine who cut off her glorious long hair to buy a watch chain for her lover. Who sold   or at least pawned   his watch to buy his beloved a comb to hold her glorious long hair.

Not that her hair is or ever was long. Or all that glorious. But she does feel awfully naked on her shorn side, without the earclips. Lopsided, as her hairdresser had said. She could kick herself for not daring to wear them in the street, while she could still have hidden them under hair, if she felt too self-conscious. A provocation to muggers.

She's lucky that whoever held the iron bar against the door didn't let her come inside, & hit her over the head with it. There definitely is more than one bright side to this robbery.

Which she nonetheless reports to the police. After pressing money into the super's theatrically protesting hands.

Two policemen are sitting in her kitchen when her dead mother's plagiarist (?) makes his daily call. She tells him what happened. & that whoever stole her mother's make-up case also stole her mother's manuscript, which she'd been keeping in it.

Upsetting him greatly. Does anyone else know about the manuscript's existence? Other than herself? Had she told anyone about it?

She tries to reassure him. New York thieves weren't interested in literature. & they certainly didn't read Czech. Whoever took the manuscript took it only because it happened to be inside the mother-of-pearl make-up case.

Maybe she'd get it back, if the police caught the thief. Or thieves.

There were two policemen sitting in her kitchen that moment. She needed to get back to them.

He is reluctant to let her go. Does she promise to call him back as soon as they leave. Collect, like the first time?

She will: she says.

He's still upset   & wide awake   when she calls back at 9 p.m. Which is 2 a.m. in Prague, in the wintertime. —He has also been drinking.

Did they catch him? he asks, instead of saying: Hello.

Not yet.

What if the thief knows how much that manuscript is worth to him? & blackmails him? Or threatens to expose him? For something he didn't do! Why didn't she mail him the damn thing when she received the earclips, as he had trusted her to do? Why hadn't she simply burned it? He would have trusted her not to hold her dead mother's manuscript over his head for the rest of his life.

Which is how he feels now. What he fears. That he'll never be free of it. No matter how many other books he may write. Books that haven't the slightest connection with anything related to the life of the dead Mara Pandora.

About whom he had actually wanted to write. An insider's biography. From the point of view of her ghost. Who is reluctant to pass on to higher realms. & is furious that her books have died with her, although delighted to be outside an old body racked with pain.

Attracted by the smell of vodka in his glass she hangs from the ceiling fixture of her old bedroom, at night, explaining the craft of writing, style, & the ever-changing fashions of reality, in the light of her literarily lived life.

But how can he write that now! When he has to be afraid of anything that links his name to hers.

He sounds so worried, she wants to tell him that her mother's manuscript wasn't stolen. For the simple reason that it never existed. That she has been trying to create it. Painstakingly. For the last three months, taking directions from his fat boy. That she invented the manuscript's existence on a hunch. In anger, after reading about herself changed into a fat boy. Whom he made less intelligent than she used to be in those days. But why should she jeopardize a translation-free future.

—& his trust!

His lack of cool surprises her. It doesn't match his photograph. But then, she has not experienced homelessness. In the sense of rooflesssness. She doesn't know how it feels to lie down to sleep somewhere outside, in some public place. In any weather. At the mercy of probing nightsticks. & pranky street kids. & pissing dogs. At best. Until that afternoon she had felt totally secure in her snug Village apartment.

Which has now been invaded. Through the tiny garden she loves so much. She now feels exposed through her kitchen window. Watched by whoever knew where she kept her few valuables, to find them so quickly, & hardly make any mess, during the fifteen minutes of howling alarm. —Which the robber(s), not she, must have set off when he/they entered, seconds before she came home.— Now she's afraid to open the blinds, to look at her Rose of Sharon.

Which she tells him. Including the recent onslaught of the ominous little black birds.

His anxiety disperses at the sound of hers. He has been selfish, worrying only from his end. Anticipating the worst. Which only brought it on sooner: he says. Sounding like Milosz on the train to Paris. All the more since he's saying it in Czech.

He's glad she didn't get hurt, at least. & that the translation wasn't stolen also, after all the work she put into it. He's understanding her dead mother better & better, worrying about the safety of unpublished manuscripts.

Still, she shouldn't give those silly black birds too much credit. Black wasn't an ominous color. It was the color in which all colors slept: he says. Echoing the chimney sweep from Staten Island. He's not only the literary executioner of her dead mother, & her own fat past, he's also a ghost spooking into her PAPER HAREM.

He's so sorry that she was stripped of her diamonds. So soon. He had hoped they'd make her forget her childhood earaches. —& should, incidentally, net that thief a couple of thou.

He also knows how valuable that amethyst ring was. From her mother, who used to tell him that wearing amethysts inclined one toward chastity.

The loss of a warm coat   at the threshold of winter was a nightmare of the homeless. & an experience he wishes on no one. His misery never wanted company.

But his success does. He'll take care of her, when he comes to New York: he says. Unexpectedly switching to fluent, almost accentless English.

Which makes her wonder what exactly he means by: He'll take care of her. Which has no ominous double meaning in Czech. If that's why he suddenly switched.

Of course he may not know that it has one in English. He may have switched only to impress her. Or to let her know that he'll be able to check her translation, & make sure she didn't substitute her own novel of revenge.

It will certainly be interesting to meet him: she says.

He looks forward to meeting her, too.

She's burning her no-longer-needed attempts at recreating the repulsive teenage Mara/Cornelia in her livingroom fireplace   which the building management would prefer her not to use; they don't like to have the chimney cleaned for a rent-controlled flue   when Mandy Murdoch knocks at her door.

How did he get inside the building?

Somebody was coming out; he let him in.

She doesn't like that. She doesn't like that at all. Visitors were supposed to ring the bell, then identify themselves through the intercom. She was robbed a couple of weeks ago. She doesn't want strangers wandering around the building.

He's sorry she was robbed. But he's no stranger. —& he's bringing her something that ought to pick up her spirits. She needs to come away from the fire though. What he's bringing her isn't fireproof.

Another article to translate?

No, not another article. She'll see. & she'll be pleased.

Fine. Then he'll have to wait a few minutes.

He struggles out of a new-looking wintercoat, hampered by his radio, which he changes from one hand to the other to get out of the sleeves. She asks him to: Turn it off. She needs to concentrate.

She needs to concentrate? On burning papers?

Yes. She's calling forth the evil spirit who stole her diamond earclips.

WHO stole her diamond earclips?!

There's something in his tone that makes her turn around & look at him, now nestled into the far corner of her couch. The suit he's wearing also looks new. Could he ... Could a pear like him climb into even a groundfloor kitchen window, six some feet above garden level?

—Shame on you, Mara. Suspecting an old pear that has been irritating you for over twenty years. You're getting paranoid, see-sawing between victim & schemer.—

If she knew she wouldn't need to call him forth: she says.

How does she know it's a he? Some thieves were women. —She doesn't really believe in that hocus-pocus, does she?

Fire was a powerful element: she says: & hers was a special fireplace. When Milosz built their first fire, after they moved in she sat down in front of it, & said: House, tell me your story. Without giving much thought to what she might be conjuring up. The next thing they knew was that she had unsettled a ghost. A bony old Italian woman named Grace. In a dark-blue dress with dark-green trimming around elbow-long sleeves, who had lived in the apartment after the house was built by her husband in 1832.

Grace started haunting her dreams, making noises in the kitchen, misplacing knives & breaking cups. Finally Milosz built another fire, & made her ask: What Grace wanted.

& Grace told them: She had died unexpectedly, of just a little chill. There had been no time to administer last rites. Now her soul couldn't cross the threshold into Heaven.

Milosz suggested that they go to a church in the neighborhood, & burn a candle for Grace's soul. They did, & on their way out, on the church steps, she found a dark-blue silk kerchief with dark-green roses. She still has it somewhere in a drawer.

Might it not be possible that Grace, who was obviously grateful for having been released from her ghost status, would take time off from her heavenly duties, & help her find the thief?

Mandy Murdoch loves ghost stories, but that doesn't mean he believes in them.

He's also wondering if that old boyfriend of hers still has keys to her apartment. Maybe he came by to reclaim those diamonds, after he unexpectedly ran out of money. Or into another woman. & while he was at it, he helped himself to whatever else she had that looked valuable. After all, that guy knew what she had better than anybody.

He's returning her narrow look. He obviously doesn't like Milosz much. He may also be trying to refocus the suspicion he may be reading in her eyes. Especially if he is reading through guilt-framed glasses.

She doesn't answer. She sits down next to him on the couch & asks: Well, what has he brought her?

He doesn't want her to think that he's a translation

charity case: he says. Ceremoniously extracting ten new
$100 bills from inside his new-looking suit. Fanning them
out under her nose. Counting: One two three four
five six seven eight nine ten. Now will she
translate his article!

Where did he suddenly find a thousand dollars?

He took her suggestion. He got a job.

Doing what?

Oh, sitting in a chair behind a desk in an empty lobby,
from 10 p.m. to 6 a.m. He's a night watchman.

Really? For how long has he been doing that?

Oh — Since the day after she told him to get a job.
However long ago that was. It's not too bad. He can read.
Sometimes he even writes a little.

Does he wear a uniform?

Yes.

& carry a gun?

No. No gun. Although he's been thinking of getting one.
Of applying for a permit. A gang of young punks almost got
inside the other night, scaring him half to death. Luckily he
managed to let the iron gate down in time. He thinks he
may have squashed a few toes.

Really? What kind of building is he watching?

Oh, some warehouse. They manufacture paper, he
thinks.

In Brooklyn?

Yes, in Brooklyn.

& he starts at 10?

That's right.

Shouldn't he be on his way then? At a quarter past 9?

Not on a Tuesday. He's off on Tuesdays. & he wants to
take her out to dinner. To that same expensive place she
took him to.

He's certainly had a change of life!

She can say that again. & it's all thanks to her!

—Are you paranoid, Mara? Or getting your degree in criminal psychology?

A familiar smell assails her, as she walks into her editor's office to deliver her finished translation. On deadline day. Her olfactory memory identifies it as *Monsieur* by Rochas, which her grandfather used to wear; in discreeter do(w)sage. It rises like an aura from the black-leather back in the visitors' chair, across from her editor.

Who calls out her name: Ah, Mara Pandora. Prompt as always.

The black-leather back springs into the air, & her dead mother's plagiarist(?) rushes to greet her. Arms spread wide, & beaming, he plants two kisses on her cheeks.

Which grow rigid. A reflex to the grandfather's perfume, which scares up the teenage Mara, cringing away from kissing him goodnight.

She thinks: What a deep impact her mother must have made on this young man, for him to be wearing the grandfather's perfume.

He looks more attractive than the jacket cover. Which does not do justice to his eyes. They are the eyes of a Douanier Rousseau jungle beast. A deep rich gold around a center of shiny black vigilance.

He is older than his photograph. Still, he must have been in his teens when her mother picked him off the street.

At last! he beams. Unfastening two diamonds from his right ear, & transferring them to hers. To compensate for her recent loss.

She can also have three, & he'll keep two, depending on

how she feels about odd & even numbers.

She says: He's overwhelming her. She's very happy to have two. He has restored the balance of her haircut.

On which he compliments her.

Leading her by a hand he seats her in the visitors' chair. Which is still warm from his body heat. So warm it penetrates her heavy black-leather pants.

Their   mildly astonished   editor calls to his assistant to: bring in another chair.

No need. No need. Writers spent their lives sitting in chairs   hunched over papers. They ended up looking like questionmarks. He prefers to stand.

In front of the window, slightly behind the editor's right shoulder. His eyes can look straight into hers. & they do, with a glittering, almost hypnotic intensity.

Which may be lack of sleep. She doesn't think he takes drugs.

He's pulling out a pack of Vlasta, offering them around. She accepts. The editor declines. & calls to his assistant to: find an ashtray somewhere.

Are they ... related? he asks pensively. He thinks he detects a decided resemblance.

She thinks that, to a pudgy, balding family man in a grey suit, with a red tie, they probably look like members of a black-leather tribe, who decorate their ears & outrage their hair. —Unless all Czechs look alike to Non-Czechs ...

She says that: She feels flattered. Her eyes are half as big as his. —Hoping he doesn't hear it as the double meaning she did not intend.— Instead she has a bigger nose.

Her dead mother's plagiarist(?) starts lavishing praise upon her nose. Such an interesting aristocratic nose. Such dramatic flaring nostrils. Does she take snuff?

No, but she has allergies that keep her sneezing.

He laughs.

The editor is looking at her nose. Pensively. Trying to justify the enthusiasm of this good-looking, best-selling young author.

Who is enthusiastically assuring him that: Of course they are related. All authors were related to their translators. Who clad their words in new   often more becoming dress. Sharing words could be more intimate than sharing a bed.

She protests. Laughing. She thinks translators were eaten alive by their authors.

She's making him feel like a boa constrictor.

The editor laughs: He hadn't realized translating was so painful.

It was an exercise in self-effacement. —Although, not in his case. In his case she'd felt an instant affinity with his style. & a strange familiarity with the subject matter. Translating this book sometimes felt as though she were writing her own story.

She's playing with him. She's having fun. But he is not amused. His eyes have grown darker. Holding hers in a vise. She sees fear in them, & a warning. Maybe he thinks that the theft of her dead mother's manuscript was a lie. —Which it was, of course. But not the lie he thinks it was.— Maybe he's expecting her to pull the manuscript out of the enormous black leather bag in her lap, at any moment, & show it to the editor.

Who says: Well, whatever their relationship, he trusts that it will be a happy one. They're particularly fortunate in that this particular author speaks magnificent English   as surely she must have noticed   & will therefore be able to go over the translation himself.

She turns to ice. She feels like snatching up the stack of papers from under the editor's nose, & tearing them to shreds, & throwing the pieces into his fatuous fat face.

How fortunate indeed! she coos, in sudden Oxford British. Perhaps the author will start going over her work right then & there, while she gratefully sits by, eager to hear his improvements.

What has he said to offend her? asks the editor. Nobody is disputing her conscientiousness. Still, it seems to him that they should all take advantage of the presence of an author who knows English. & obviously knows best what he wants to say.

Her dead mother's plagiarist(?) feels no need whatsoever to read over a translation by Mara Pandora before the book comes out. When he'll be delighted to read it. For pleasure.

She smiles at him. She almost blows him a kiss. Then glowers at the editor, who looks taken aback. She feels him wonder why this attractive, successful young author, this bright new star in the literary firmament, is deferring to his translator. Courting her almost. A woman at least ten years his senior, when he doesn't even look like a young man who is particularly interested in women. —Unless young men who look like he looks aren't gay, in Czechoslovakia.

Actually, the editor is pondering the art of asskissing without making contact. Something he often ponders when he first meets a new author. Especially a new foreign author. New foreign authors normally express boundless gratitude to their editor. Who brought them to America. & might possibly help them to stay in America, if their book is a success. For which they're also grateful to their editor.

Rather than to their translator, whom they normally suspect of diminishing them. & quibble with, even beyond page-proof stage, if they know English at all. Especially if they know very little English. Which is why editorial policy normally frowns on bringing authors face to face with their translators.

To whom they normally do not offer diamonds.

The editor ponders if a transfer of diamonds constitutes contact. Or, on the contrary, avoidance of contact. In the latter case he wouldn't mind having a little attention directed toward his own naked ears. He wouldn't mind being offered the third diamond, for instance. He probably wouldn't wear it, but it would make a nice present for his wife. Who'd be too self-conscious to wear it but happy to pass it on to their daughter. Who'd eventually be forced to hand it over to her brother. That way, everyone in the family would have gotten a diamond. & the ears of this abnormal pair would be equalized.

The editor wonders if they belong to some international underground. A sexual, rather than a political underground, he hopes. & the newly arrived author expects to be introduced to the New York branch by his wretched translator.

—Who moonlights as a *maîtresse*. A term the editor just picked up from another young author he's publishing. A New York author, who needs no translation, thank God. & should lure even the couch potatoes into reading him, with his whiplashers & chainslingers, who'll torture them to ecstasy.—

That could explain the misplaced generosity of this bizarre young man. Who even wants to split his American royalties with his translator.

He asks her: Does she know that this generous young author is offering her 50% of his American royalties?

That's what he told her.

He told her? When?

On the telephone.

Oh ... then they know each other. (Now, that explains a lot.)

Her dead mother's plagiarist(?) says: They're old friends, at the very moment she says: They just met. In the editor's office. But they've frequently spoken on the telephone: She quickly adds.

About the translation?

Yes, of course.

But ... they did know each other before?

No.

But ... How did they get hold of each other? The editor is sure he didn't tell the author who was translating his book. & the author was not only unlisted, but unapproachable by telephone. Even to his editor, who'd had to cable him & ask him to call him, collect, every time he needed to get in touch with him.

The eyes of her dead mother's plagiarist(?) are commanding her to: Let him handle this! When she sees the birds again. Falling from the sky, outside the editor's window. In the middle of Manhattan. She hopes she's not the only one to see them, & points, crying: Look! Look!

The editor says that happens every year, at the onset of winter. He'd been shocked, too, the first time he saw them. By the sheer mass of them. Now he knows they're on their way to a warmer climate.

Her dead mother's plagiarist(?) says that: To him black has always been a good omen.

He's smiling, but his eyes are ominous. They are definitely warning her. There still is fear in them, but there's something else beneath the fear. Something that's not fun to play with. The crazy determination of a homeless man ready to defend his wintercoat. Or the button that came off it.

He knew perfectly well why he switched to English, for the first time in their many conversations, to tell her that: He'd take care of her when he came to New York. He will murder her, if she threatens his original authorship.

She can see the headlines:
WRITER STRANGLES TRANSLATOR to avenge his book.

Writers from all over the world will swarm to his defense, & keep him out of jail. & he'll collect the full 100% of his zooming royalties.

Critics throughout the US, Canada, & England will find fault with her faultless translation. & speak of 'A beautiful story, butchered by the terse staccato style imposed upon it by the deceitful translator'.

... When not one of them reads Czech.

The editor will remind him that he had been given the opportunity to check the wretched woman's work before they published her butchered version of his story. Which he sincerely regrets, even though it had certainly not stood in the way of sales.

He'll write other bestsellers, which he translates himself, like his fat boy. Or writes directly in his magnificent English. & there will be no end to his glory.

Or, he'll never write another book, on the contrary. & drink up the fortune he made on the two Mara Pandoras. Stealing from the mother, & strangling the daughter. Years go by, & a janitor finds an old drunk dead in some fleabag hotel in New York, or Chicago, or New Orleans. A corpse propped against a headboard, with the clippings of his forgotten fame neatly laid out around him on the bedspread. Which is alive with roaches.

Or he's found in a gutter. With his clippings neatly

stored in a plastic bag. His story will be revived briefly. &
his strangled translator blamed for the tragic decline &
premature demise of a promising young talent. & that will
be that. & still no one will have checked her translation
against the original.

Which a graduate student in philology eventually does.
Ten, or fifty, or a hundred years later. For his/her thesis.
He/She can't believe that a translation that has the exact
flavor of the original became a cause for murder. So he or
she starts digging for other causes. & discovers that the
strangled translator had a mother by the same name, who
wrote novels. In one of which a daughter had also been
strangled, although by her mother.

The murderer-author seemed to have lived with the
novelist-mother for a period of years, until her death,
before he wrote this, his first book. Etc. Etc. Eventually the
student arrives at a conclusion that is not too dissimilar
from hers, when she first read the book. & vindicates not
only her faultless translation, but also her suspicion of
plagiarism. Which vindicates her mother, & resurrects her
as a writer.

Which no longer matters to either of them. But matters
to the student, who graduates with honors.

Meanwhile her dead mother's plagiarist(?) is telling the editor that every writer in Czechoslovakia knew of Mara Pandora's superb translations into English, & hoped to get *her*, & no one else, to translate his/her work.

Therefore, when his book was bought in America, he wanted to make sure that she was going to be his translator. He easily found her name in the New York Telephone Book & called. Ready to plead with her, if necessary.

To their mutual joy, she told him that his manuscript was sitting on her kitchen counter. She had just started working on it. & very much enjoyed his style.

The frowning editor interrupts to say that company policy rarely permitted authors to choose their own translators. In the interest of the book. He therefore shares in their mutual joy. A felicitous coincidence.

He also congratulates her on being so well known in Czechoslovakia. He hopes it will not inflate her fee.

She wants to tell him that he can go delete himself! That she'll never do another translation as long as she lives, if her dead mother's plagiarist(?) comes through with his many promises. Or else, the threat she thought she read in his eyes.

She'll certainly never translate for the editor again, after his suggestion that an author go over her work. After the years of novels she has translated for him, when he just met the author, & has no idea if he can write the magnificent English he speaks.

Although she suspects that this particular author probably can. That his interest in languages & translation is genuine. He may even mean what he is now saying.

Deploring the second-fiddle role of translators. Who need to suspend their own stylistic likes & dislikes, & pledge allegiance to the idiosyncrasies of another.

How few people realized the in-depth knowledge of two languages, at least.

Seven languages, in the case of the exceptional Mara Pandora.

With whose theory: That the ideal translator picks up the writer's intent at pre-expression stage, to re-express it, in the writer's style, in the other language he enthusiastically agrees.

She's surprised. She never advanced any such theory to him, yet that is exactly how she translates. Especially in the case of idioms & word plays. That's how she arrived at: PARIS UNDER THE WEATHER ...

She smiles at him, her fears abating. He's certainly promoting her. As he said he would. He's showing her that he's keeping up his end of their bargain. & that he expects her to do the same; without playing games.

The editor is leaning forward in his chair, one hand pressed to his discreetly yawning mouth. Away from this stream of unsolicited testimony to the translating experience.

Which her dead mother's plagiarist(?) is wholeheartedly recommending to all writers concerned with language. It will lead to a more conscious relationship with their own language. It will deepen their psychological appreciation of syntax & grammar, as they consciously use the subjunctive to express fear or desire. It will sharpen their awareness of structure.

He, for one, is planning to add translating to his

experience with language.

Is he really! —The words fall out of her mouth before she can catch them.— In that case, how would he like to start with an article. From English into Czech. 24 single-spaced pages. It has already been paid for, but she'd be glad to pass the work & the money on to him.

He says: He'll be happy to do it. If she's sure she doesn't want to do it herself. Is there something she dislikes about the way it's written?

The man writes like a pear. Besides, she's through with translating. His fat boy was the highpoint at which she intends to stop.

The editor assumes that this must be a passing phase. Why would she be so self-defeating, stopping at the height of her acclaim. Disappointing all the authors in Czechoslovakia. —What else does she want to do?

He is looking at her with a certain curiosity. She feels him wondering if she's making a lavish living, as a *maîtresse*, in the sexual underworld of New York City. But his curiosity vanishes as soon as she says: She's writing a novel. MY PAPER HAREM. What does he think of the title?

The editor thinks: Hm ... Yeah ... Well, sounds sexy. —But, speaking of titles: THE MAN WHO USED TO BE FAT sounds like a diet book.

She typed up a list of titles: she says: IN THE SHADOW OF THE FAT BOY   THE FAT BOY'S SOUL   HIS SOUL STAYED FAT ...

The editor objects to the word SOUL in the title. It would turn off the very readers this book is aiming to attract.

Her dead mother's plagiarist(?) suggests: FAT SKELETONS.

The editor likes that. A lot. A lot better than anything he sees on her list.

So does she. He really *is* original: she says to him. Hoping to reassure him, before she takes her leave.

She's sitting in the back of the bus, on her way home, asking herself if she invited trouble, when she invited her dead mother's plagiarist(?) to translate Mandy Murdoch's article.

—Now he has a reason to come to her apartment. & he'll probably need her Czech typewriter to translate on. Unless he brought his own. Which she doubts. He doesn't look the typewriter-carrying writer type. & may wish to translate in her kitchen. He'll have plenty of opportunity to check out all her windows & doors. —The kitchen window where the burglar(s) climbed in.— & will know how to get to her, or at her, if he feels threatened. Which he seems to feel at the slightest provocation. She's certainly not going to play any more games with him, after that lethal look in his eyes. Maybe he does drugs after all. Or maybe her mother used to rub in his dependence on her, & he's making sure the daughter isn't going to do the same.

Of course he'd be coming to her apartment anyway, sooner or later. To pick her up for a dinner, or bring her back from one. Even without the excuse of Mandy Murdoch's article. —Which is probably self-sentimental treacle; she's glad to be off that hook.— He doesn't trust her enough to ignore her existence, now that they've met. To treat her like a normal author would treat a normal translator, who has finished her job. After months of long-distance telephone intimacy, while she was working on it ...

When she sees Milosz getting on the bus. A decidedly

older Milosz, with a head full of tight, shockingly grey curls.

She wonders how grey she'd be, without the jet-black dye her hairdresser smears all over her top, every two months. She hasn't seen the roots of her hair in years. Has she aged as shockingly to him, in the over twenty years they haven't seen each other?

During which they never ran into each other, though they continued to live in the same city. She assumes. In the same neighborhood, for him to be taking the same bus to go home.

He has to be going home, with the small schoolboy, whose hand he is holding.

Who looks exactly like him. Ridiculously like him. As though he had reproduced himself without anyone's assistance. Or interference. A male-virgin birth.

Except that the tight curls on the little head are blond. The halo-shade of blond, which centuries of fair-minded painters curled around the heads of angels.

Little Milosz   probably Little Miles   is dropping coins into the fare box, gently monitored by his father, in the same fantasy English he spoke over twenty years ago. Bringing angelic smiles to the seat-entitled faces of the senior citizens who crowd the front of buses at the same hour of the afternoon as home-making fathers, or mothers, collecting their first-graders after school. As translators returning from meetings with their editors, & unexpected authors.

She makes herself small, in her seat, hoping that he'll stay up front & won't see her. She has no desire to coo over Miles junior. Or listen to Miles senior explain his former life away. Denouncing the selfishness of considering oneself the living end. When life was meant to be an endless succession of smaller selves. Who brought meaning & joy, as one watched them grow. Often beyond one's own envisioned size.

Nor does she wish to be called upon to justify her diamonds —which suddenly zoom into her consciousness; pinching her right ear— or the rest of her looks. Which might look like 'not dressing her age' to a former contemporary, sedated by fatherhood.

—Milosz is heading down the aisle, pulled along by his smaller self. A fat man near her is standing up to get off. She gets off behind him.

Her walk home takes forty minutes. She spends another twenty minutes in the liquor store, stocking up, in case her dead mother's plagiarist(?) drops by to pick up his translation. She knows he likes to drink, & she might as well please him.

While pleasing herself: She has had a tense afternoon.

As she rounds the far corner of her block she recognizes the unmistakable shape of Milosz sitting huddled on her stoop. In the cold winter twilight. Without his son.

She feels like retracing her steps, & disappearing into the closest bar. But she told the man in the liquor store that she'd be home for his delivery. Besides, Milosz has seen her. He's leaping down the steps, spreading scarecrow arms in expectation of her approach.

He saw her then, on the bus. & must know that she saw him. & got off to avoid him. What does he want from her! After all these years. He has his son. Who must have a mother, even if he looks like the product of a single parent.

Would his smiling pointy teeth make her think of a squirrel now, without her mother's nasty talent for description?

He's hugging her. Demanding to know: How she has been all these many years. So she's still living in that same little apartment he found. Which turned out to have been quite a find, in retrospect. Didn't it.

He's telling her: She looks terrific! Just terrific!

She hears a touch of surprise in his voice. As though he hadn't expected her to have any looks left, after he left. But she's probably over-reacting, mishearing what may be genuine concern. & surprisingly genuine pleasure to see her.

He asks: If she is happy.

Sure. She's okay.

She doesn't feel like talking to him. What do they have to talk about, other than compare their lives away from each other. How well or poorly each of them has done. & aged. Or else regurgitate the past. Which is gratuitous, unless one writes about it. Her life with Milosz is not on her list of subjects. He's too painful a subject to resurrect.

She no longer is the Mara Pandora he lived with. But why tell him that? He'd just smile pointedly, & tell her that: She hasn't changed a bit! & expect her to go along with whatever it is he decides he suddenly wants to do. As in the past. —Like coming inside the apartment, for instance.

Which would annoy her. & might even make her angry. Enough to start flaunting her bachelor existence in his face. With asterisks to highlight particular inmates of her PAPER HAREM. In which he has no place. Except as an usher at the door.

The asterisks would probably look like little fireflies to him, signalling her continued acquiescence.

She bursts out laughing at the absurdity of it all. Besides, his sudden presence is making her nervous.

Why is she laughing?

Oh, nothing. At the absurdity of him sitting on a cold stoop in the middle of winter.

He didn't feel cold, waiting for her.

Well, he should have. She has no warmth left in her. For him.

She didn't mean to say that kind of thing. That's why she didn't want to talk to him. He looks surprised. Not offended. Not hurt. Surprised. He always thinks warmly of

her: he says: & often. He often worries that she's not eating
right, with no one to cook for her.

She stares at him. Thinking: What about your little son?
What about your little son's mother? Who's probably
supporting you. Is she American? Or Czech? Or something
totally other. Samoan, maybe. Are you married to her? &
what about the others in between. Do you have warm
thoughts for all of them?

Why isn't he mentioning his son? He knows she saw
them together on the bus.

Maybe he didn't see her. But felt her presence. & finally
gave in to the longing he'd felt for her all these years.

Tears start rising in her eyes. She instantly censors them
with a cough. Cut out this nonsense, Mara! What do you
think you're doing! Letting yourself be drawn back into his
net, by the delusion of your own magnetic pull.

It's comforting to be thought of warmly: she says: But
she's catching cold, standing in the street. She needs to go
inside.

He moves with her, back toward the stoop. But she stops
him with an outstretched arm. Pointing to the delivery man
from the liquor store who is coming down the street like
saving grace on roller skates, clutching a case of bottles to
his prominent stomach. Here comes my delivery! she cries.
Goodbye.

Is she giving a party? He's standing two steps from the
door now, still expecting to be invited in.

No, just stocking up on translating fuel.

She gestures for the man to go in, then goes in after him.
Leaving Milosz standing on the stoop. Goodbye, nice to see
him: she calls again, as the door falls shut behind her.

She has poured herself a Bourbon, to reward & to console herself for not letting Milosz come in. She'll drink it in a nice hot tub, where she can drown the stupid delusion that he still loves her. & feels as baffled & disconcerted, still standing out there in the street, maybe, as she felt when she found his wedding announcement stuck to the bathroom mirror.

How strange that the   no-longer   young man her mother had hate-named The Squirrel had reappeared the same day   moments after   she met the strange young man her mother had perhaps loved.

Who feels less of a stranger to her   despite her earlier fear fantasies about him   than the grey-headed Milosz with a child by his side. Which has removed him from their age group, & turned him into a patriarch. An untouchable, like her grandfather.

He has to have seen her on the bus. & came to challenge her avoiding him. He still can't tolerate it when she acts on her own.

& is now ringing her doorbell.
Just as she's about to step into the tub.
She puts her robe back on, unable to resist the call of the world outside. While muttering that: He can ring until his finger freezes to the button. Until the neighbors phone the police, & he is carted away. He's not coming inside her place! Even if he did find it.
Maybe he has come to ask for it back!

Who is it? She barks into the intercom, wondering if he'll offer to come in & make goulash & dumplings for her, like for the women editor. & what she'll answer if he does.

She's not prepared for the voice of her dead mother's plagiarist(?) apologizing for descending upon her like a swarm of blackbirds. He tried to call, but he had no change. So he took a cab, hoping to find her home. If she's busy he'll just pick up the translation she offered him, & go away again. If not, he'd like to take her out to dinner. If she's willing. & hungry.

She's not dressed. & was about to take a bath. But he can come in; at least for a drink.

He looks pale. Like a tourist from Transylvania. Bourbon in hand, he stalks about her apartment, inspecting everything in close-up, like a cat. She wonders what animal her mother would have picked for him. Had perhaps picked for him? Something feline & black. Maybe an owl. His eyes are enormous.

He wants to see her garden, but the door has been sealed for winter. She throws the outside light on, & he recognizes her naked Rose of Sharon through the kitchen window.

Is this where the robber climbed in?

Everything is exactly as he pictured it: he says contentedly, settling onto the couch.

She refills their drinks. Doesn't he ever sleep? she asks.

He operates in forty-eight-hour shifts, then conks out for twelve to twenty. He has sixteen more hours to go.

Would he like to see the article?

Sure.

He starts reading it. Stopping to laugh. Now he knows how a pear writes. With its stem. He's laughing. At his own joke, or at the article.

Which he'd love to start on right away. Does she mind?

Not eating dinner? He feels caught in the pear spirit. Perhaps, with the help of a few more bottled spirits ... Does the Pear drink?

He sure does.

He knew it. He writes like a sentimental old souse.

She leads him to the Czech typewriter in the kitchen. —Just like her mother's old work horse. Did she bring it with her from Prague?

No. The Pear found it for her, to put the proper accents into his article. She sets the bottle of Bourbon on the counter, within his reach. She'll take her bath, then, & just go to bed without supper, like a punished teenager.

He who sleeps dines: He laughs, echoing her proverb-loving grandfather.

She falls asleep to the sound of frantic typing. Hazily thinking that she's inviting her murderer to strangle her, as her grandfather claimed murder victims often did.

& that Milosz would be there to protect her, if she had let him come in.

But then, Milosz would strangle her soul, without leaving fingerprints around her neck.

It's bright daylight when she wakes up. The sound of typing is still coming from the kitchen. As is the smell of coffee. She goes to meet it, & finds her dead mother's plagiarist(?) still hunched over the typewriter. In leopard underwear, with naked, work-glistening torso. His earclips & a heap of gold chains are lying on the kitchen counter, between a coffee mug & the empty Bourbon bottle.

—Her mother used to discard all her rings & bracelets   even her support stocking   so that nothing would dam the flow of words.

He has almost finished. Almost. Almost.

He made coffee; he hopes she doesn't mind. He found everything right away. In the same places as in the kitchen in Prague.

The coffee he made tastes better than what she makes, with the same ingredients. She lights one of his Vlasta that are lying on the counter.

He gestures for her to help herself. He gesticulates. He mutters. He types like one possessed. Suddenly he stops. He has finished the article. Can he read it to her?

He reads for over an hour. His sentences flow. His words sparkle. She hasn't read the original, but the translation is a moving elegy of an expatriate who found a new art form in America.

She's impressed. It's splendid: she tells him: She'll write him a check right away. She thanks him for letting her off the Pear hook. It would have taken her at least a week to do those twenty-four pages. She has no enthusiasm left for rewording other people's words. She asks if he wants to go out for lunch, or wait till dinner.

He doesn't hear her. He has passed out. His head is hanging way over the back of the typing chair.

Which has coasters. She rolls his comatose body into the living room. Bumpily, across two narrow thresholds. She tilts the chair & he spills onto the couch. He falls gracefully. Even with his eyes closed he reminds her of a jungle beast. His face has the deceptive tenderness of a big cat. A leopard, since he's wearing those shorts.

She places a kiss on the leopard's nose. —Surprising herself.— Then gets the quilt from her bed, & covers him up.

She gathers his discarded clothes & jewelry, & places everything neatly on the typing chair beside his head. She gets his cigarettes & an ashtray, & places them there, too, in case he wakes up.

If what he said is true, he won't for the next twelve to twenty hours. She decides to treat herself to lunch. Uptown, at the Museum, where she hasn't gone in years.

She stays out until seven. Reluctant to walk in on him, & wake him up. She's no longer afraid of him, but she doesn't know how leopards wake up.

He's in the bath tub, & calls for her to fix herself a drink. To come on in, & keep him tub company. He used to do that with her mother. —Whom he'd have to lift in & out of the water, toward the end.— Her mother loved to lie in a warm tub, with a slow drink in her hand. & him sitting on the edge, talking about God knew what. Solving all the problems of this polluted world.

How come he's up? He said he conked out for at least twelve hours.

The jet lag, probably. It was after all five hours later in Prague. —Did she put him on the couch, & spread the quilt over him? That was really nice of her. He slept so well. He feels like a new person.—

Why doesn't she come in. Come on in. Fix herself a drink, & renew his while she was at it.

She doesn't particularly wish to play her mother's role in reverse: she says. —Nor does she particularly wish to stare at an underwater penis. Which she doesn't say. She could stare at his face. Why does she need to stare at all.

Okay. He'll come out then. Does she mind if he wears her robe? —& she's mistaken if she thinks of her mother as a repulsive old woman. Her mother's flesh never sagged, & her stomach never stuck out. It was as though her body froze under the shock of her accident. It never changed. Except that the slightest movement seemed to hurt her, toward the end. Especially at night. He'd crawl into bed with her then, & talk her to sleep.

She shudders. She would have had to wrap herself in Saran Wrap, to lie down next to her mother.

She can't bring herself to ask: If he had loved her mother. Made love to her mother. Isn't he gay?

He emerges from the bathroom, sleek in her black silk robe. Which looks better on him than it does on her. —Without the grandfather's overpowering perfume. Instead he's overpowering her with her own Joy, by Jean Patou. The 'most expensive perfume in the world'. She buys herself a small bottle as a reward, every time she gets paid for a translation.

She tells him: He looks & smells like an improved version

of herself. Before she asks: If he'd mind not wearing *Monsieur*. At least not around her. She still cringes at the smell of her grandfather. Who used to cook the food that used to make her fat.

He looks amazed. He thought she'd adored her grandfather. That she'd loved him so much better than her mother.

She had loved nothing & nobody, during those horror years. Including her fat self. Just like his fat boy. She thought he knew that.

He does. In theory. But he guesses he doesn't really. Hasn't she been slender for over half her life. Was it true then, that teenage fatness shaped your self-image for the rest of your life? He hasn't had the experience. He grew up scrawny. He never had that much to eat. Maybe he'll get fat now, & still think of himself as thin. & write another book about that.

Of course he'll switch perfumes, if it's that psychological with her. He adopted the grandfather's perfume only because he'd found a large bottle, still unopened, in his room when he moved in. & her mother had liked him to wear *Monsieur*. Maybe they can pick out something together. Something they both like, on their way to dinner. Because tonight they'll finally eat dinner. Where does she normally go?

She says: She normally doesn't eat dinner when she has eaten lunch. She's still watching her figure. But tonight she'll make an exception.

Good. He'll watch her figure for her.

Which reminds her. She has been meaning to ask him. Does he sew? She means: Did he do all that stitching over the diamonds on the black bra he sent her? & how on earth did he get hold of her exact bra size?

He didn't. That was one of her mother's bras. But, yes, he did the stitching himself. Rather neatly, doesn't she think?

Oh no. She has been wearing one of her mother's old brassieres!

Not an old one. A brand new one. One her mother had just had made. & never worn. & she needn't be so squeamish about her mother's body. Hasn't he just told her: Her mother kept her shape to the very end. Why can't she let go of the ghosts, & live with the living.

Very well. What kind of food are the living in the mood for? Italian Chinese Burmese Janice's Fish House. A French diner that's open all night.

Yes.

Which one?

The French diner. Then they can sit & talk all night, if they feel like it.

Will he pass out on her again?

He won't. What's the matter with her. If she isn't hating the past she's dreading the future. Has she maybe studied Arabic? In which two present tenses consist of the just ending past & the just about to begin future?

No. Has he?

He's learning it. He wants to meet some Arabs in New York.

A teetering Mandy Murdoch bumps into them on their way out the door. OOOPS! Ex——cuse him: He stutters. Staring at their ears. He has come to inquire about his article.

Behold The Pear: she says. In Czech.

Her dead mother's plagiarist(?) extends an enthusiastic hand, expressing his pleasure & the honor to meet the author of such a fine article.

Which is finished! She'll run back in & get it.

Her dead mother's plagiarist(?) will get it. He'll get it. If she'll just give him her keys.

Mandy Murdoch didn't know she had a younger brother. Living in New York. So it had been her brother who borrowed her diamonds, & now they're wearing them in shifts.

He might have called: she says sternly: Instead of barging in on her all the time. & isn't he supposed to be at work. It's not Tuesday.

At work? Oh … Uh … Those hoods came back, & this time he wasn't able to lower the iron gate. They got inside & vandalized the place. He was lucky, they ran right past him. He can't live that dangerously, at his age. He quit.

—What does she think of his article?

It reads well in Czech.

As well as in English?

She doesn't know. She heard it only in Czech.

What does she mean! She translated it!

No, she didn't. Her brother did.

What does she mean! He trusted *her* to do it! & no one else. He paid her to do it. In advance.

She passed the money on to her brother.

But he wanted *her* to do it! After all the trouble &
hardship he went to, to get those thousand bucks for her.

What trouble & hardship?

He told her: That life-threatening job. —Her brother
doesn't know him. He seems nice enough. & his English
sounds good. But he doesn't know where he comes from.
He's too young to understand how it feels to lose a dear
talented friend, whom you've known for over twenty years.

He's wrong about that. Her brother has had many losses
in his life. Including the loss of her mother, whom he
lovingly cared for until her death.

Her brother also happened to be *the* best-selling author in
Czechoslovakia at the moment. His name as the translator
will assure his article prominent publication. & God only
knew what else besides. More money, probably. He should
consider himself most fortunate. —Besides, the translation
of his article sounds better than anything she's heard of his
in English.

She doesn't mean that!

Of course she doesn't: smiles her dead mother's
plagiarist(?), who has returned with the translated article.
Reaffirming what a pleasure it was to make the
acquaintance of the author. He feels as though he knew him
intimately, after translating him: he says.

Should they invite The Pear to come along for a drink?
He asks her in Czech.

She shakes her head. She's had it with him. Besides, she
has the unpleasant suspicion that it was he who robbed her,
back in August, to pay her to translate his article.

In that case, shouldn't they get him drunker still, & find
out?

What for? That stuff must have been sold & resold a
thousand times.

Yes, but they might retrieve her mother's manuscript. &

burn it in her fireplace. Along with their distrust of each other.

He really needn't distrust her. Not any more.

Mandy Murdoch says: If they're going to continue to speak their private language, he thinks he'll go home.

Her dead mother's plagiarist(?) loves the French diner. &
the waiters & everyone who's eating there at 10:30 at night
seems to love him. He's funny. & quick. Almost
unbearably ingratiating. She can't remember laughing so
much with anyone in her PAPER HAREM.

Or with Milosz. Whose sudden reappearance as a ghost
in winter twilight has shrunk to a fatherly eunuch playing
peek-a-boo, in her laughter-loosened mind.

Her dead mother's plagiarist(?) wasn't lying when he told
her that he was the redeemer of literary child abuse, the first
time they spoke on the telephone. His joyful, up-beat
presence is taking the weight off her past.

He has ordered champagne. He wants to ask her
something conventional, that will be less embarrassing to
ask with a conventional glass of champagne in one's hand.
Would she be willing to marry him?

But——isn't he gay?

He is by preference, but not exclusively. & since when has
being gay stood in the way of a nice conventional marriage.
Besides, his question has no sordid ulterior motives, like
copulation. Or the occasionally related urge for
procreation. He simply wants to stay in America, & have
the right to work there legally. He wants to we(l)d two
rituals of bureaucracy: Marriage & a green card.

She doesn't know. She needs to think.

That's what she always says. He's not such a bad bargain.
He can cook. & clean. —& sew.— & he'll keep her
laughing. Is there anyone in her life she likes better than
him?

Not really. Not at the moment.

Good. Nor is there anyone in his.

No one he likes better than himself? Is he a Leo, to be so self-loving?

He's Scorpio. Can't she tell? He has the typical Scorpio eyes.

His eyes aren't typical of anything. They're extra-ordinary.

Good. Will she marry him then? They'll ask the editor & The Pear to be their witnesses, & make the announcement on the day their book comes out.

The Pear thinks they're brother & sister.

He does! Then he'll be witness to their incest. That should occupy his drunken old conscience & inspire another moving article, comparing them to the pharaohs.

What about the house in Prague, if he doesn't go back. The grandfather's store. He can't just walk away from it all!

Why can't he? She did. —But he didn't. He hasn't told her yet. The place has become The Mara Pandora Foundation. A small retreat for writers to spend from one month to a year completing a project. Up to six writers at a time. It's supported by the City, which pays a cook & his nephew to take care of the maintenance. He'd thought of reserving that job for himself, initially. But that was before he sold his book to America.

The sewing machines in the old workroom have been replaced by two word processors & four self-correcting electric typewriters. The store has become a kitchen, the bar, & a communal diningroom. The upstairs floor is now all bedrooms.

He supervised the reconstruction before he left. & earned much praise for his 'generous gesture'. Which saved him a mint in taxes. This way   who could tell with poli-tics   they might both have a place to go back to, in

Prague, some day, if they should feel like it. So, what does she think?

She doesn't know. She needs to catch her breath. He certainly works fast.

When he's inspired. He gets intuitions. Suddenly something tells him exactly what to do. —Like marrying her.— He has been training his receptivity. Learning to trust it when it happens. She should trust it, too. So far it has brought nothing but good results.

She needs to sleep on it.

He already slept on it. On her couch. That's when he got the inspiration to ask for her hand in marriage. But he'll sleep on it once more. With her. & program her dreams. So she'll wake up, & turn to him with a smile, saying: Yes, be my house-husband. My ghost slayer. My weight lifter. My detoxifier of maternal venom. I've always wanted to know Arabic. I want to study it with you.

She smiles at him. She holds her hand out across the table.

There is a fresh graffiti on the warehouse wall outside the French diner, directly under a street lamp. It says: DON'T BELIEVE THE HYPE. DEAD PUSSYCATS CAN TAKE CARE OF THEMSELVES. SIGNED: FAT BOY.

He reads it, & wishes he'd seen that before he finished the book. Maybe he'll take it up to the editor, to add to her translation. Just that paragraph, by itself, on the last page. With an asterisk, giving credit to the walls of New York City.

If he does, his posthumous fans will accuse his translator of inflating/sabotaging his   by then classic   terse staccato style.

He laughs. He won't let them. After he finishes her mother's biography, he'll write IN DEFENSE OF THE ART OF TRANSLATING. A PROTEST! Now, will she marry him?

She smiles. She takes his arm. They pick their way across the sticky cobblestones of the meat district, softly discussing plans for ever-closer best-selling collaborations.

DON'T BELIEVE THE HYPE. DEAD PUSSYCATS ARE DEAD BECAUSE THEY COULDN'T TAKE CARE OF THEMSELVES. SIGNED: FAT GIRL